STARGΛTE

SG·1 ™

THE ILLUSTRATED COMPANION
SEASONS 5 AND 6

STARGATE SG-1: THE ILLUSTRATED COMPANION SEASONS 5 AND 6

1 84023 606 X
Diamond edition: 1 84023 722 8

Published by
Titan Books
A division of
Titan Publishing Group Ltd
144 Southwark St
London
SE1 0UP

First edition June 2003
2 4 6 8 10 9 7 5 3 1

DEDICATION
This book is dedicated to Philip, Kerry and my SG-1, Stuart.

ACKNOWLEDGEMENTS
As always, I am eternally grateful to all of the brilliant people who work on *Stargate SG-1* in Vancouver. I have no space to mention them all individually but off the top of my head, thanks to Tracy who always answers the phone as if she was waiting for me to call; Len who offers the best transport in the business; Jack who feeds me vast quantities of chocolate cake and noodles (not together you understand) and Rick Dean, who always laughs at my jokes and is even more enthusiastic about the show than me, and, of course, Barry, who gives great hugs. Special thanks are due to Sue, Richard, Katy and Jaclyn for their help with the episode guides and quotes, and to Kim Cowan and Bill Vigars for taking good care of me on set. Adam Newell at Titan Books is truly fab and has the patience of a saint. Thanks a lot one and all! — Thomasina Gibson

Titan Books would also like to thank all the *Stargate* cast and crew members who kindly wrote pieces for this book. We're grateful to Charlie Clementson and Kobie Jackson at MGM for their continuing help. And thanks again to Richard Pasco, for the pictures from *Gatecon* 2002 on pages 153-154.

Did you enjoy this book? We love to hear from our readers. Please e-mail us at:
readerfeedback@titanemail.com or write to Reader Feedback at the above address. To subscribe to our regular newsletter for up-to-the-minute news, great offers and competitions, email: titan-news@titanemail.com

Titan Books' film and TV range are available from all good bookshops or direct from our mail order service. For a free catalogue or to order, phone 01536 764646 with your credit card details, or write to Titan Books Mail Order, AASM Ltd, Unit 6, Pipewell Industrial Estate, Desborough, Northants, NN14 2SW. Please quote reference SG/C3.

A CIP catalogue record for this title is available from the British Library.

Printed and bound in Great Britain by MPG, Bodmin, Cornwall.

STARGÅTE

SG·1 ™

THE ILLUSTRATED COMPANION
SEASONS 5 AND 6

Thomasina Gibson

Stargate SG-1 developed for television by
Brad Wright & Jonathan Glassner

TITAN BOOKS

Contents

Foreword

Hello gentle readers. Welcome to the third indispensable *Stargate SG-1* companion. (I have never written a Foreword for a book before, so bear with me!) This is a wonderful opportunity for me to share with you the magic that is *Stargate SG-1*. This is more than just a television show. Well, that's not entirely true... it really *is* just a television show, but for those of us who work on it, it's a family. It's a magical, crazy, surreal, laughter-filled house peopled with strange and amazing creatures... most of them human.

I have been a part of this family since 12 February 1997, when I arrived in Vancouver, British Columbia. I was a fresh-faced young upstart, full of high hopes and great expectations. I was also scared out of my tree. I was about to embark on an adventure, the likes of which I had never experienced — the making of a science fiction television pilot. All I had to do was keep my nose clean, remember my lines and play nice in the sandbox and hope, really *hope*, they wouldn't kill my character off.

Thankfully, the Powers That Be didn't kill off Samantha Carter,

Daniel Jackson, Teal'c or General Hammond. We were off and running on what promised to be a two year... four year... five year... six year... and oh my goodness *seven* year marathon (so far!) of whacky, fun-filled adventures. We've made a lot of friends and enemies along the way. Some have stayed with us, from Janet Fraiser, the ultimate healer and goddess of all that is medical, to Apophis, the ultimate villain and god of all that is false. (Is he dead yet?) We now have bigger, meaner fish to fry. The Replicators... oh how I hate bugs! And Anubis — he truly is evil personified. I could go on, but I don't want to scare you away from the rest of this book...

We've met great allies. The Tok'ra, who saved Jacob Carter's life and made him the ultimate ambassador. (I, for one, was and am exceedingly pleased by this plot twist.) Then there's the Asgard — those cuddly, grey skinned, bulgy-eyed masters of supreme being. And the Nox: what's not to love about those straw-haired cuties? And there's many, many more.

Samantha Carter? Well, she's loved (and lost) some great fellas. Martouf (yes, OK, she killed him), Narim (granted, she ran off while his planet blew up), her ex-fiancé Jonas (alright, she would have killed him... but instead she settled for watching him plunge to his death), Ambassador Joe Faxon (I know, she left him to die with the Ashen), Orlin (true, he re-ascended... I suspect it was to get away from her curse!). I could go on, but this is getting far too depressing. Don't get me wrong though, I personally have had a *blast* playing Carter!

Ah, but back to the magic that is *Stargate SG-1*. We really are a family. The cast and crew really do love each other. We really do have a lot of fun... day in, day out. Rain or shine, or sleet. We laugh. Every day. Really... we do! It's hard to pinpoint what makes this show work. I think it's the chemistry between all the people involved. We have an amazing creative team. We have a cast, helmed by Richard, who love what they do, and love to laugh — loud and often. We have an exceptional crew of warm, funny, hard-working and exceedingly talented people. Coming to work is a pleasure — we *really* enjoy making this show. Above all else though, we have a legion of the most incredibly supportive fans. Never forget how much we appreciate you. Never forget how much we acknowledge you. For without you, we would not be here. Simple as that. So, thank you from the bottom of our hearts. Enjoy this book!

My personal thanks and love,

Amanda Tapping

The Journey Continues

Amanda Tapping

"It's hard to believe we've gone six years since we shot the pilot. I don't feel any older!"

I t has indeed been six years since Brad Wright and Jonathan Glassner created the wonder that is *Stargate SG-1*. Always innovative, always fun, the show has been the perfect foil to some of the more pretentious offerings on our screens. Now under the auspices of Wright and Robert C. Cooper, the show continues to go from strength to strength. Speaking of the previous two years Cooper says, "I think it's gone very well. At the end of season four it was like, how are we going to do season five and make it better? But by the end of it, I thought the fifth year was our best ever. So we asked ourselves the same question when we got to season six!"

Wright chips in with, "I honestly didn't think we were going to do a sixth season. The problem was that we needed to find a new broadcaster. Fortunately, the SCI FI Channel stepped in with an offer to pick up the show." Delighted to have acquired *Stargate SG-1* for their impressive portfolio, Bonnie Hammer, President of SCI FI Channel announced, "We are thrilled to be able to strengthen our already solid relationship with MGM by adding *Stargate* to our stable of original series. With its stellar creative team, we are confident that the series will soon build upon its already loyal audience." Ms Hammer was right.

Robert Cooper is please to proclaim that "our ratings have consistently increased to where we've got a '2' at the end of the year, which is pretty much the highest rating the network has ever had! So that's all good for us." The show is successful the world over, and so popular in the UK that SKY One tags new shows, including the much vaunted *Enterprise*, on to the end of *Stargate* to encourage new viewers. That's quite ironic, especially seeing as the visual effects of the *Star Trek* show's pilot episode sneaked the Emmy award for Best Visual Effects from *Stargate* effects producer James Tichenor and his team. Says Cooper, "Our VFX got nominated, but you can't compete against a pilot. We get $400,000 an episode but pilots get millions, so our guys deserve a pat on the back."

Executive producer Michael Greenburg is also justifiably proud of the work produced by the special FX team led by Wray Douglas. "These guys keep coming up with tons of great stuff, but they really did us

Above: The cast, out of uniform for once.

proud, along with the art department, in 'Frozen'. We were supposed to be working in sub-zero conditions, so we brought in big refrigeration units to lower the temperature — so that we could see our actors' breath! Then Wray found this wonderful artificial snow we'd never seen before, which apparently had the same consistency as the snow found in Antarctica. The SFX and the art departments came up with a set that looked *totally* believable."

As well as introducing new types of effects, *Stargate* took the brave step of introducing a new cast member, to bring SG-1's team complement back to four after the departure of Michael Shanks at the end of season five. Corin Nemec stepped into the breach. Executive producer John Smith admired the subtle way in which the actor became accustomed to the role: "He was a little uncomfortable at first, because he felt very much like the new guy. But within a few episodes he really settled in a little bit better, and found his character. I think he's done great."

The same can be said of new writer, Damian Kindler. Kindler had already worked with Robert Cooper on the highly successful *Psi Factor: Chronicles of the Paranormal*, back when they both lived in Toronto. "Being taken on as a staff writer on a show as fantastic as *Stargate SG-1* rates as one of the pinnacles of my career," says Kindler. "I was over the moon when they rang and offered me the job." Welcoming him into the fold, co-producer and fellow writer Joe Mallozzi says of the latest recruit, "We're looking forward to a Kindler, gentler *Stargate*." (For more from Mr Kindler, see below, where he has kindly given us his advice for established writers who want to pitch for the show.)

As the cast and crew approached what was not only the end of the season, but possibly also the end of the show, Richard Dean Anderson expressed his feelings towards that eventuality: "During one of my conversations with Brad Wright, I remember saying to him that if we all walk away at the end of this sixth season, we can all be very proud of what we have accomplished, both creatively and on a business level."

The man who started the whole shebang agrees: "I'm as pleased with this season as with any season of *Stargate* we've ever done. What makes me most happy is that after all this time, we're *still* fresh creatively. Added to that, our set has a terrific energy, and is a great place to hang out — and that's something to be proud of at the end of six years on any television show!"

As it turned out of course, six years wasn't the end: *Stargate SG-1*'s journey was far from over…

How to Pitch the Perfect Script
By Damian Kindler

Whichever show you choose as the platform to international fame and fortune, the first thing you have to know about pitching a script is this: coming in to pitch as a freelancer is a *very* different experience to pitching stories when you're on the writing staff. Both experiences are unique, and as different as night and day. However, for those intrepid souls determined to embark on this journey of discovery (and believe me, that's exactly what it is) here are my tried and tested tips for freelance pitchers. Good luck.

Rule 1: Do Your Homework. You must know the show. I've seen quite a few freelancers come in after me, and they didn't even get their feet in the door, because it was obvious that they just did not know our show, other than in a cursory way. Nothing is more embarrassing than when a writer, who may well be a great writer, pitches ideas that are either episodes we've done (and we've done a lot of great episodes), or

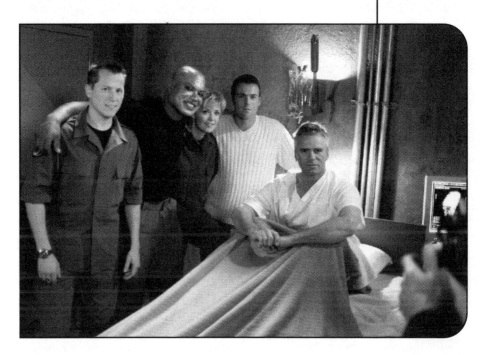

episodes that we would never do. "Let's do a werewolf story!" Sorry, we don't *do* that — go to *Buffy*. So homework's important. It's a 'Catch-22' situation, because you have to pitch something fresh and new, but nevertheless offer a story that makes sense within the world that's been created. The only way you're going to achieve that is to do a lot of research, and spend a huge amount of time at Gateworld.net!

When I was invited to pitch, I watched more than twenty of the most recent episodes of *Stargate SG-1*, I read lots of scripts, I read the *Illustrated Companions* and detailed synopses from the Internet. It took me months to get up to speed, just so I could think about what story to pitch. It's a lot of work to do on the possibility of maybe selling one story! You have to take a big shot at it. Once they say, "Would you, sir, like to come inside the Pearly Gates?" then you must do a massive amount of work to prove that you are well schooled in the show. Even then you're not completely ready, because there will be gaps in your knowledge. It's up to you to continue to plug those gaps.

The other thing to keep in mind is that pitching to a room full of people is quite unnerving. It's *scary*! In my case, it wasn't so much because of the people — Rob Cooper, Brad Wright, Peter DeLuise and Rick Dean Anderson all made me feel very welcome — but I didn't want

Above: Say cheese! Gathering for a snapshot, during the making of 'Abyss'.

to let anybody down. I'd known Rob for a long time before I attempted to pitch to the *Stargate* producers, and I didn't want to embarrass my friend. Luckily, I didn't make too much of an ass of myself, and everybody really responded to that.

Rule 2: Flesh Out The Story. Don't come in with just a little sentence, like 'Teal'c and Bra'tac get ambushed' or 'Teal'c and Bra'tac get ambushed by women' (they wish). That's a Chris Judge pitch. He pitches that every time I see him. He says, "Hey, Kindler — how about writing Teal'c gets ambushed by women?" (Actually, Teal'c *is* going to get ambushed by women. Chris is writing an episode called 'Birthright' where exactly that happens. But hey, back to the creative process.) You must pitch a well-formed, well-rounded idea and it must be clean and clear. You must pitch something about a page and a half long, with a heading that goes something like this: 'SG-1 is babysitting a team of scientists, who are gaga over the fact that they are being babysat by their heroes. Something happens and SG-1 gets kidnapped. The scientists, being fools, decide to use some form of technology, ie ring transport, to go after them, only to realise that SG-1 got captured on purpose. They are on an undercover mission and now they have big problems.' So there you go — you have to see the story turning into something, but you're not finishing it off. You're giving the Powers That Be the opportunity to

say, "Yes, we know exactly how we will progress this story!" You're giving them a nice menu detailing what the show is, but you don't have to offer the dessert, or tell them how well the meat is cooked. You must say, "This is my idea" — and let it go. Let them take the idea, make it their own and give it back to you, because at the end of the day, you are writing for their pleasure. (OK, and their money.)

Above: Wardrobe supremo Barry Peters (right, with Peter DeLuise, left) takes control of headgear.

Rule 3: Listen To The Powers That Be. If they give you a note, or an idea, or an opinion, it must go into the intake valve, stay there, gestate and come out again in what you hand back to them. You do *not* say, "Well, that's an interesting opinion Mr Wright: I'll take it under advisement, but I'm going to do my own thing." Nothing despoils the well more than ignoring a note from Brad or Rob, because they know what they want. They appreciate it when their notes are taken and added to. So, no going it alone, and input said notes into your product.

My last piece of advice is simply this. If — and that's a very big 'if' — they do accept your pitch, it's *not* cool to yell "Ohmigod!" and jump up and down. Brad doesn't like people jumping on his couch, and neither does Rob. So you may want to wait until you're in your car before flipping out. I know what the euphoria feels like, and it is wonderful. What's *so* wonderful is that it's reserved for the very special few. An elite group of which I'm proud to be a member." λ

Enemies

Regular cast: Richard Dean Anderson (Colonel Jack O'Neill), Michael Shanks (Dr Daniel Jackson; season 5), Amanda Tapping (Captain Samantha Carter), Christopher Judge (Teal'c), Corin Nemec (Jonas Quinn; season 6), Don S. Davis (General Hammond), Teryl Rothery (Dr Janet Fraiser)

Story by: Brad Wright, Robert C. Cooper, Joseph Mallozzi and Paul Mullie
Teleplay by: Robert C. Cooper
Directed by: Martin Wood

Guest cast: Carmen Argenziano (Jacob/Selmak), Peter Williams (Apophis), Jennifer Calvert (Ren'al), Gary Jones (Sgt Davis), Thomas Milburn (Jaffa), Dean Moen (Jaffa)

After blowing up Vorash's sun, obliterating the bulk of Apophis's fleet, and losing Teal'c — who is presumed dead — the rest of the team find themselves stranded, along with Jacob Carter, hundreds of light years from home. Worse still, they're in a stand-off against the mighty Apophis. The only communication from the System Lord's ship leaves SG-1 in no doubt that Apophis intends to eliminate his enemies once and for all. He is about to strike when another ship arrives, and attacks the Goa'uld. SG-1 board Apophis's apparently deserted ship, and while they try to salvage parts, they quickly discover the reason for his hasty retreat — Replicators. Our heroes find themselves in a race against time to find the crystals necessary to repair their own ship whilst evading the marauding creatures. Matters only get worse when Teal'c returns...

> **O'Neill to Carter**
>
> "He's looking a little pissed."
>
> "We did just destroy his fleet."

"This is the one where we end with Teal'c saying he's Apophis's boy!" director Martin Wood recalls. "The interesting thing in this one, is that all of the ships you see are actually just one set. Apophis's Teltak, and the Peltak on the ship that we're in... and I'll explain the significance of that later...

"The main thing I remember is the hand-held running and gunning sequence. See, I had designed a shot: the idea was to run the camera straight at Rick [Dean Anderson], who was gonna start shooting. Then he spins around, and we see what he's shooting at, then we run with him straight at Michael [Shanks]. Then behind them, more bugs are coming, and they are shooting down at them. That was all done in one shot. When you see the finished episode, look for it,

because it's spectacular! Though they ended up cutting away to the bugs on the wall, which I think was a mistake, because you can't see that the shot was all done in one."

Above: Teal'c returns to the Dark Side.

The director reveals that the incendiary aspect of the weapons used in the show was very real: "The camera operator had to be decked out in body armour, because he was very close to these guns. He had a face shield, helmet, all the stuff! So he was protected, but the walls of the set were made of Styrofoam, and the concussion from the shots actually moved the walls and created Styrofoam dust. As we're running you can see this white dust on the corner of the floor, and actually falling out of the walls as the Styrofoam grates against itself. It was hysterical!"

Another of Wood's favourite shots was in the ring room, when SG-1 are about to bid their farewells: "There is a shot in the ring room with Rick sliding on the floor, and he blasts a bug just as he gets into the rings. That's the end of my shot, and the reason he did what he did was because the ring room was exactly the same on both ships. It's the same set! In order to make it look like something different was happening, I had to find something that completely covered the frame — and we used the bug. So that very dramatic shot was born from having to use the same set, and not being able to ring out and ring into it." ʎ

Threshold

Written by: Brad Wright	Guest cast: Tony Amendola (Bra'tac), Brook Parker
Directed by: Peter DeLuise	(Drey'auc), Peter Williams (Apophis), David Lovgern (Va'lar)

Although free from the influence of Apophis, a brainwashed Teal'c still believes himself to be the First Prime of his god. SG-1 decide to call in the big guns, in the shape of Teal'c's former mentor Bra'tac, to help convince the mentally disturbed Jaffa that Apophis was indeed a false god. Bra'tac decides that the only course of action is to deprive Teal'c of his symbiote and invoke the ancient 'Rite of Masuraan' — a ritual which allows Teal'c to re-live his painful past in the hope that he will once again see the truth and denounce his allegiance to Apophis and the System Lords. Unfortunately, the Rite is a kill-or-cure process and SG-1 and the rest of Teal'c's friends can only stand by and hope he chooses Life...

Daniel to O'Neill

"Did he just call me a woman?"

"I believe he did."

"Obviously delirious."

Tony Amendola says 'Threshold' is one of his favourite episodes: "It's intriguing because the writers all see different things in Bra'tac's character. Chris [Judge] writes from inside the relationship, while Peter [DeLuise] has his own slant, which is also fascinating. Brad Wright developed the character, and really writes incredibly well for Bra'tac. He did a tremendous job with this episode."

Displaying his love and knowledge of *Star Trek*, director Peter DeLuise begins, "We were in a little bit of trouble there at the start of season five, though we were a lot cleverer than the *Voyager* crew, because we managed to get back home in just one episode. Teal'c had been brainwashed by Apophis to believe that he was still his loyal servant, so we had to de-program Teal'c — all in forty-eight minutes! We had a lot of fun with that, because Brad Wright had the clever idea of taking Teal'c and bringing him close to death in the Rite of Masuraan. We could then see Teal'c's life pass before him at the moment of his death to find out what was real and what was not real." Modest to a fault, DeLuise continues, "We saw these wonderful — if I do say so myself — flashbacks of Teal'c when he was in the service of Apophis, moving up through the ranks from a warrior/grunt/private

to a lieutenant-type and ultimately to First Prime status. We also see the wonderful Bra'tac in his former role as Apophis's First Prime, and it was a lot of fun to shoot that."

Above: Teal'c and Drey'auc re-live fond memories.

Part of the episode was shot in hills above Vancouver — in the snow. "Chris Judge was a really good sport because he had to be top-less," praises DeLuise. "He had been working out during the off-season and he was in prime fighting condition. He really put it all out there and kicked major butt in that episode." The director insists that any complaining from the delicate Mr Judge was kept to a minimum, and jokes, "We had a few cries of 'I'm freezing!' and 'I'm getting frost-bite!' But we just ignored him."

DeLuise is also quick to praise director of photography Peter Woeste, who came up with a distinctive look for the flashback sequences. "You'll notice that it was very saturated with sort of a blue tinge to it," DeLuise says. "That was all Peter Woeste's idea. A lot of the time I get the acclaim for things that Peter has actually come up with, so I have to pass on the credit where it's due. He came up with the design, and I thought it was amazing." Å

Ascension

Written by: Robert C. Cooper Directed by: Martin Wood	Guest cast: Sean Patrick Flannery (Orlin), John de Lancie (Colonel Frank Simmons), Ben Wilkinson (O'Brien), Eric Breker (Colonel Reynolds), Rob Fournier (Special Forces Commander)

O n a routine mission, the team find a planet apparently devastated by a Goa'uld attack. While investigating what seems to be an alien weapon, Carter is rendered unconscious. Back on Earth she seems fine, medically, but insists that she has been visited by Orlin, an alien whom no one else can see. Until her actual state of mind can be clarified, Hammond puts Carter on sick leave. At home she tries to determine the alien's intentions, and is given a frightening insight into what really took place back on the stricken planet. Meanwhile SG-16, under orders from the Pentagon and the President, re-visit the planet in order to fire up the weapon. Orlin tells Carter that the weapon could spell disaster for the human race, and that the test firing must be stopped at all costs. Clearly besotted with the good major, Orlin prefers to place his life on the line rather than endanger hers.

Carter to O'Neill

"So far he's only shown himself to me."

"Maybe he's shy."

"I really wanted to do an old fashioned romantic comedy, but of course we had to add a sci-fi twist," executive producer and writer Robert Cooper explains. "This is a sci-fi series after all! We rarely get to go home with the characters and see where they live, but 'Ascension' gave us that chance. We were very lucky to get an actor of the calibre of Sean Patrick Flannery, who brought a completely unexpected level to the character of Orlin. Amanda won a well-deserved Leo award as

Ascended Beings

Orlin's race of highly advanced beings has extraordinary abilities, including the power to make themselves invisible. They can take on human form, although this particular feat saps their energy and limits their powers. Though they can choose to return to this mortal coil, they cannot re-ascend without collected assistance from others of their kind. Generally considered to be a benevolent people, they can seriously kick butt when circumstances dictate!

Above: The things you can make with string, a piece of gum and a toaster…

lead actress on the strength of her performance in this show. I think we fill her full of techno-babble so often that we forget she is a truly gifted actress, capable of really 'bringing the funny' when she's asked to. The scene with Teal'c and O'Neill at her door with the pizzas and videos is still one of my all-time favourites. Not just for the *Star Wars* reference and the cowboy hat, but Amanda's performance as she plays not only the discomfort at the prospect of having Orlin discovered, but the whole does-she-or-doesn't-she want O'Neill to think she has a man inside. It's great multi-level comedy acting."

The 'Carter at home' segments of the episode were filmed in a private residence on the outskirts of Vancouver, and contained lots of personal items specially imported by Amanda Tapping from her own home. "This house was lovely and very Sam, but I wanted to add some really personal touches. The photos you see are my own. There's one of my twin and me as babies, and some of my relatives including my grandfather. I've been given some lovely gifts by fans of the show over the years and wanted to show some of them, too. So the quilts you see thrown over the chairs, and the candles dotted around have been brought from home and are my way of thanking the fans for being so gracious. It's not much, just a gesture. Just my small way of showing my appreciation for all they've so freely given me." ⅄

The Fifth Man

Written by: Joseph Mallozzi and Paul Mullie **Directed by:** Peter DeLuise	**Guest cast:** Dion Johnstone (Lieutenant Tyler), Gary Jones (Sgt Davis), John de Lancie (Colonel Frank Simmons), Karen van Blankenstein (Nurse), Brad Kelly (Jaffa), Shawn Stewart (Jaffa), Dario Delaco (Jaffa)

G-1 are under heavy fire from the Goa'uld during a mission to P7S441. Carter, Jackson and Teal'c return to Earth and tell Hammond that O'Neill is trapped, along with Lt Tyler. Hammond demands to know just who this Tyler is, and the team are astonished to learn that no one back at the SGC has ever heard of him! Suspecting that they may be under some form of alien influence, Hammond confines them to the base while they undergo medical tests. Carter manages to hack into the base computer, and discovers that an unidentified person has infiltrated the mainframe and accessed their personal files. Colonel Simmons arrives at the base to interrogate the team, hoping to use this case of 'alien mind-control' as a reason to close down the Stargate project. Back on P7S441, O'Neill and Tyler both find out that what you see isn't always what you get.

Director Peter DeLuise describes the deceptive skills of O'Neill's companion thus: "Here we have an alien creature that has a sort of memory chameleon effect. So he's able to camouflage his way into your memory, making you *think* that you know him, when in fact you do not. The alien was played by Dion Johnstone, who has been many characters for us in the past, including Chaka in 'The First Ones' and Warwick in 'Forsaken'. Later on, in 'Metamorphosis', he again plays one of those heavily made-up persons. Dion plays aliens for us a lot of the time, so it was kinda nice that we got to see his real face in this one." Complimenting the actor, DeLuise continues, "He's Shakespearian-trained and was recently on stage here in Vancouver playing Tybalt in *Romeo and Juliet*."

DeLuise teasingly hangs his head in shame when he recounts his most vivid memory from the making of 'The Fifth Man'. "We killed a lot of Jaffa. We killed too many Jaffa, apparently," he says. "At the end of the episode there is a shot of O'Neill and the rest of the guys, walking toward the Stargate. There were dead Jaffa on the ground, because they were guarding the Stargate and there was a battle. O'Neill had to

Above: Three unhappy team members leave two behind enemy lines.

walk around some of the fellas who were dead on the ground, and I got in trouble for showing that. I had to go to the 'How come?' room for that one! The Powers That Be said, 'Why did you have him step over that dead guy?' and I said, 'It's in the script! They took care of the guards. Where were they supposed to be? Gone? Missing?' It became this big issue — I was a bloodthirsty American director who liked dead bodies everywhere!" Deeply unaffected by this slur DeLuise goes on, "If you recall in 'Wormhole X-Treme!' when the colonel played by my brother Michael DeLuise has a kissing scene with the alien princess, he says, 'There's all these dead bodies here. I can't have a kissing scene with all these dead bodies!' That was a direct result of the issue in 'The Fifth Man'. The way they decided to deal with it in the end was by zooming in on the shot of O'Neill stepping over the Jaffa, so that you couldn't see what he was stepping over."

Asked if there really is a 'How come?' room, DeLuise replies, "Of course! If the Powers That Be want to know 'How come you did this?' or 'How come you did that?' — you have to step into the 'How come?' room. They don't have a 'What were you thinking?' room on *Stargate*, because it would be too big. The 'How come?' room is a manageable size." ⋏

Red Sky

Written by: Ron Wilkerson Directed by: Martin Wood	Guest cast: Fred Applegate (Elrad), John Prosky (Malchus), Norman Armour (Dr MacLaren), Brian Jensen (Freyr)

SG-1 are mistaken for elves, and welcomed as messengers of the gods by a society of gentle souls on the planet Katal. But within moments of their arrival, the sky takes on an eerie red glow. One of the village elders declares this to be a portent of doom and insists these guests are harbingers of evil. The elders visit the Hall of Wisdom where a pre-recorded message from their god, Freyr, convinces them that this is indeed Ragnarok — the end of the world. Carter confesses that she did bypass some of the normal dialing protocols in order to gain a lock on the planet, and surmises that their wormhole passed through the system's sun, causing the anomaly. SG-1 manage to establish direct contact with the Asgard, who are protectors of the planet, but they seem unwilling to help save the inhabitants from destruction...

O'Neill to Carter

"What just happened?"

"Some sort of shift in the light frequency."

"Good — I thought I was having a stroke."

Martin Wood directed 'Red Sky' and begins, "When they first presented it to me they said, 'We're going to build this little town as an indoors set,' and I said, 'Why are you going to build it indoors?' and they said, 'Because we want to have control over the colour of the sky.' That sounds weird, but there was a good reason: they wanted to do all sorts of colour changes in the set (which was, incidentally, a very expensive and beautifully done set — the production design team really went for it). When you have a scene which goes from an outside location to an indoors set, or vice-versa, it's always a problem to make the light look natural in the indoors set. This episode has the sky turning red and all that, but we could change the lighting easily, because we were actually shooting the outside inside, if you see what I mean." Of course we do.

"I really wanted some nice big trees in there," Wood continues, "because you can't convince me that this is a little village without some trees. I also wanted to see evidence of animals around, for example horses that would draw carriages and such like. There is one shot where we come out from behind a big tree and we hear the sound of a horse and wagon

coming through, and you glimpse the wagon, and then you see SG-1 walking towards us. That was actually done by 'Evil' Kenny Gibbs and Dave Sinclair, the two props guys, pulling a wagon across the set. The rest of us were shouting, 'Faster you mules, get out of the shot!' It was all part of trying to convince people that we're outdoors."

Another memorable moment is the initial shot of coming through the Gate from SG-1's 'POV' (point of view), when they tumble down. "Originally the script said something like 'they come through the Gate, hard'," says Wood. "I thought that if there was something wrong with the Gate, then it should *look* like there was something wrong with the Gate from what we see on screen. I said to the cameraman, Will Waring, 'I'm going to throw you through the Gate and you're gonna come up and land, shooting all the while.' He said, 'Do I have to?' but he went and got all padded up. He didn't quite throw himself, but sort of tumbled through, holding a teeny tiny camera which made it look as though he were falling all over the place." The extra effort made for a very effective shot. λ

Above: Three elves and an alien.

Story by: Heather E. Ash **Directed by:** Peter DeLuise	**Guest cast:** Colleen Rennison (Cassandra), Jacqueline Samuda (Nirrti), Richard de Klerk (Dominic), Karen van Blankenstein (Nurse)

Fraiser and Carter's adopted daughter develops more than a case of teenage tantrums when a dormant retrovirus, introduced by the Goa'uld Nirrti, begins to take effect. Set to kick in once a child reaches puberty, the virus invades Cassandra's body, which starts to burn up under the strain. Nirrti is forced to give up her cloak of invisibility in order to retrieve a sample of Cassandra's blood, and is captured. She offers to help the child in return for her freedom, clearly wishing to continue her experiments in another part of the galaxy. However, the System Lord has vastly underestimated the power of a mother bear protecting her cub, and must battle Fraiser for supremacy over the young girl's health.

Hammond to Nirrti

"I should remind you that the woman holding the gun on you is Cassandra's mother."

Although kids do change as they grow up, Cassandra underwent a *complete* change of body and personality in this episode. Katie Stuart had originally played the character in the episode 'Singularity', way back in *Stargate*'s first season. Stuart was unavailable to reprise the role, so the producers returned to Colleen Rennison, the girl who admirably soaked Daniel Jackson in season two's 'Bane'. Peter DeLuise explains, "Everyone thought Colleen had done such a great

Nirrti

Hindu Goddess of Darkness, Death and Destruction, this deity has an equally nasty masculine side called Nirrta. Tossed out into the wilderness for treachery against the Goa'uld and every other race she's encountered, the steely-eyed Nirrti has developed stealth capabilities, allowing her to become invisible. Determined to create a super-being for her symbiote, so that she can attain even greater physical strength and longevity, she relentlessly continues to experiment on individuals who are often unaware of her nefarious purpose. Devious enough to conceal her experiments as well as her presence, Nirrti has planted a plethora of neurological 'time bombs' within her subjects. Having travelled extensively throughout the galaxy, the range to which her destructive strategy extends has yet to be established.

job for us previously, and we were looking for a way to get her back. This was the perfect opportunity."

Teryl Rothery really relished the chance to show Janet Fraiser in a different light. "'Rite of Passage' will certainly be up there on the list of my Top 20 favourite *Stargate* episodes," she emphatically declares. "It was just so much fun to make. We see another side to Janet, which I loved playing. I call it the 'momma bear syndrome'. You don't want to mess with this woman when it comes to her cub, Cassandra. Nirrti found that out the hard way! It was also the first time in five years we see that Janet does, in fact, have a home," the actress continues. "She doesn't live on the base after all. And in that home, she's not only dealing with a teenager with raging hormones, but a teenager from another planet that's been messed about by a Goa'uld. Whew!!

"This episode was especially fun due to the fact that I was also filming my 'behind the scenes' footage for the MGM Home Entertainment DVD. Check it out. Thomasina Gibson came up with the idea and I loved making it, but once you watch it, you'll understand why I'm an actress and not a documentary film-maker…" ⋏

Above: Daniel is happy to let Carter take control.

Beast of Burden

Written by: Peter DeLuise	Guest cast: Larry Drake (Burrock), Dion Johnstone
Directed by: Martin Wood	(Chaka), Alex Zahara (Shy One), Vince Hammond (Big One), Noel Callaghan (Boy)

Whilst conducting an anthropological study, Daniel sees his friend Chaka being captured by some men, and taken off through the Stargate. Insisting that it's his fault for teaching the Unas to trust humans, Daniel persuades General Hammond to mount a rescue mission. Following Chaka, SG-1 discover a race of people who keep the Unas as slaves, using them literally as beasts of burden. Understandably unhappy with this state of affairs, O'Neill and Daniel try to free the enslaved creatures, only to end up imprisoned themselves. Carter and Teal'c must come to the rescue…

"This was a really cool episode," states writer Peter DeLuise. "We see Chaka again! Dion Johnstone is back, revisiting the character he originally played in 'The First Ones' [in season four]. We find that Daniel has been keeping track of the Unas because they are worthy of study. When he sees Chaka being abducted, he feels really guilty, and thinks he's responsible. So Daniel enlists the help of the rest of the team, and they go to this other planet where they find that Unas are used as slaves. But there's a bit more to it than that. SG-1 find themselves right in the middle of this undesirable world of humans — who were originally oppressed by Unas. The humans were used very much like the Jaffa are used today. They were controlled by a System Lord, and were oppressed by the Unas, but once the System Lord left, the Unas's structure fell apart. The human 'slaves' then triumphed over the Unas, because they were slightly more intelligent than their masters. But they weren't *that* much more intelligent, because they then made the Unas *their* slaves, as beasts of burden.

"This was my slavery allegory," DeLuise continues. "I really liked the episode because we didn't have a clean 'what's the right thing to do here?' This was a complicated issue, in that it wasn't 'straight' slavery *per se*. There's also a big dilemma here: if we give the Unas a way of freeing themselves, it means a lot of people are going to get killed! We end up basically giving the Unas a way of defending themselves

— but at what cost? Chaka, not being born into that sort of social order, immediately recognised that it wasn't cool to be imprisoned, to have his freedom taken away from him — so obviously he wanted to free his fellow Unas. This wasn't a very neat ending. It was very much a 'what have we done?' kind of a thing. I really liked that it was very thought-provoking, because it touched on the issue of our right to interfere. In *Star Trek*, it's very clear. You don't go out to mess with a society — the Prime Directive states that you can't do that. On *Stargate* we break the Prime Directive every week! This particular case is a good example of where a prime directive might have helped us out." DeLuise feels 'Beast of Burden' is an episode that shows *Stargate* at its best: "It doesn't bang you over the head with a message, but it still felt very strong to me. Brad Wright was my champion on this one. When I pitched a story about Unas slavery, he recognised its value straight away, because he used to work on *The Outer Limits*, where they often tackled that kind of subject." ⋏

Above: A puzzled Unas ponders life behind bars.

The Tomb

Written by: Joseph Mallozzi and Paul Mullie Directed by: Peter DeLuise	Guest cast: Earl Pastko (Colonel Zukhov), Alexander Kalugin (Major Vallarin), Jennifer Halley (Lt Tolinev), Vitaliy Kravchenko (Lt Marchenko), Garry Chalk (Russian Colonel)

There's not a lot of *entente cordiale* between the representatives of the two superpowers: O'Neill is less than happy when he finds that he has to team up with a Russian SG unit to rescue a group of their colleagues who have gone missing off-world. Claiming first dibs, he insists on being in command of the entire group. Amid an atmosphere of distrust, both SG teams investigate a Babylonian crypt where the bodies of the missing Russians are found. Whilst Marduk, a particularly unpleasant Goa'uld, stalks the unwary wanderers, O'Neill discovers the Russians do indeed have an agenda they've chosen not to share with their American counterparts and which threatens the lives of everyone.

Daniel

"Yes, you go down the dark hallway alone and I'll wait here in the dark room alone."

Peter DeLuise reveals that "'The Tomb' is the first time we feature a Russian SG-team on camera. Previously we had shied away from that, and been very evasive. But now, based on our mutual Full Disclosure agreement, our lot had to integrate with them." It doesn't take a lot to make the director happy because he goes on, "We're renting their Stargate from them anyway (at decent rates), and we get to meet a hot Russian chick! Because of that, 'The Tomb' was a lot of fun to do."

According to DeLuise, co-producers "Joe Mallozzi and Paul Mullie came up with the idea, and it's basically the obligatory old horror movie

Marduk

According to ancient Babylonian mythology, Marduk is the creator of the Universe and Humankind, the God of Light and Life. He defeated Tiamat and Kingu, the dragons of chaos, to become supreme ruler of all. Unfortunately, a lengthy incarceration left the god so hungry he resorted to eating everything within spitting distance once released from his tomb. It's a tad less than fortunate for the humans who encounter him in this episode that Marduk's idea of a balanced diet includes people from both sides of the East/West divide.

Above: Daniel sheds some light on ancient text.

set-up, where you're stuck with people you don't trust and there's something eating you alive. That's a great formula for some fun stuff! The set was an amazing accomplishment. We had hallways with tons and tons of rocks and dirt. In every other scene, there was some guy up a ladder with a box of dirt, throwing it on us. So, yes, it was a case of Peter DeLuise's dirty sets again!" It may well have been a very dirty episode, but it turned out to be a particular favourite with executive producer Michael Greenburg: "'The Tomb' was shot by Peter Woeste and directed by Peter DeLuise, and was probably one of our most visual shows. It had a great set and fantastic lighting — a lot of presence."

There was, however, a bit of a language barrier during filming. "We had real Russians, who spoke real Russian!" says DeLuise. "They also spoke English, but with incredibly thick accents. I'd find myself saying, 'Can you be a little less Russian?' I could see them looking at me, you know — 'What do you mean, less Russian? Who is this guy?' The trouble was, for some reason — don't ask me how — in a Russian accent, the word 'colonel' comes out 'corn hole'. They came on set sounding as if they were saying corn hole and I'd be like, 'Please don't say corn hole, say colonel'. We can't have them saying Corn Hole O'Neill, because he's our hero. That was a source of great amusement, let me tell you!" ⋏

Between Two Fires

Written by: Ron Wilkerson	Guest cast: Garwin Sanford (Narim), Marie Stillin
Directed by: Bill Gereghty	(High Chancellor Travell), Peter Wingfield (Tanith),
	Gary Jones (Sgt Davis), Ryan Silverman (Tollan Guard)

S G-1 are surprised to get an invitation to attend the memorial cel-
ebrating the life of Omoc, the Tollan who seemed to have such
a low regard for human integrity. The far friendlier Narim tells
them that before he died, Omoc was concerned that the Earth
was in danger, but did not leave specific details. In a complete turn
about, the current High Chancellor offers to let Earth have access to
Tollana's weapons of superior technology. Understandably, our heroes
are wary of Greeks — or Tollans — bearing gifts,
and discover that the hand of friendship has been
extended as a trap to capture Teal'c and the rest
of SG-1, and deliver them up to an old enemy.
Unfortunately, the Tollans did not follow the old
adage — 'never trust a Goa'uld'.

Teal'c

"In order for the device to
work on both of us, we must
hold hands."

Stargate SG-1's co-creator Brad Wright has this to say about
'Between Two Fires': "I loved the moral dilemma of this episode.
Narim performs one of the most truly heroic acts we've ever shown on
Stargate. People should also know that Rob Cooper did an excellent,
and rather extensive rewrite of Ron Wilkerson's script."

For Amanda Tapping, 'Between Two Fires' was about just one
thing: Carter's Black Widow syndrome strikes again! This was yet
another episode where she loses a man. "Oh dear God, yes," she
moans. "Poor Narim." Sighing about the fact that this unfortunate
man did nothing to harm a soul she says, "I liked him, but I have to
ask you to remind people that I did not blow him up! And I do feel
pretty bad about the fact that Schrödinger (the cat) was on that planet when it blew up. You know, to lose one friend is bad enough, but
to lose two is downright careless. It was really very careless of me. Not
only did I lose one of my boyfriends, I lost my pet too! I don't know
what to say. Poor Narim was doing his best.

"I loved the joke with Narim's computer — you know — in his
house where he had the computer with the Carter-like voice. I
thought that was just hilarious." Heaving yet another sigh, Tapping
grins, "But I feel awful. I mean we just *ran*! We hauled ass! You could

Above: O'Neill and Daniel in sombre mood at Omoc's memorial.

see the look on Narim's face: 'Go! Go! Save yourself!' and we were like 'OK, see Ya!' and we were bucking it for the Stargate. We *just* get through and kaboom! It's goodnight Narim."

Lest anyone think Major Carter takes the demise of her loved ones in her stride she adds, "Of course, as a mark of respect I do light a candle for my lost ones. In fact, my house doesn't need electricity any more because I light candles for all the men I've lost. I've got the brightest house in the street. I'm like a beacon. In fact, when strangers turn up they say, 'What is she doing in there?' and my neighbours say, 'She's lighting candles for all the men she's lost. There are *thousands* of them in there.'" Oh dear! ⅄

Written by: Brad Wright **Directed by:** Peter DeLuise	**Guest cast:** Ronny Cox (Senator Kinsey), Christopher Cousins (Ambassador Joseph Faxon), Dion Luther (Mollem), Robert Moloney (Borren), Gary Jones (Sgt Norman Walter Davis), Howard Siegal (Keel), Rob Lee (Major Pierce)

SG-1 encounter a new world and a potential new ally in the war against the Goa'uld. On the surface the Aschen seem to have it all — health, wealth and happiness — and appear to live in harmony with their neighbours. However, beneath the surface — deep underground in fact — Teal'c and Daniel discover the ruins of a huge deserted city. Having studied the artifacts left by its inhabitants, Daniel realises that the Aschen aren't quite the benevolent benefactors they portray themselves as. SG-1 have yet another battle on their hands, trying to save the Earth from the formidable Aschen, and the only slightly less formidable Senator Kinsey.

O'Neill to Hammond

"These little chats of ours always bring me great joy."

This episode is the sequel-cum-prequel to one of season four's standout stories, '2010'. Giving away some of *Stargate*'s recycling secrets, writer Brad Wright admits, "Like '2010', some of the locations were inspired by the available sets we had on hand. Richard Hudolin, our production designer at the time, had designed a gorgeous and expensive set for 'Ascension' that really didn't end up with much screen time. So it became the meeting room aboard the Harvester. And the underground city in this episode was rebuilt out of the town from 'Red Sky'. You'd never recognize either one, though!"

"We meet the Aschen again," Peter DeLuise offers, "but this time we meet them (and this is weird) in what may have been the original way we met them. Or is it an alternate way? We're not sure, but either tracks.

The Aschen

A creepy bunch of individuals that make 'peaceful' contact with other races, but then destroy them from within. This is primarily done by offering medical advancements which prolong life, but leave the indigenous population sterile, and ultimately doomed to die out.

In '2010', we saw that our future characters wrote a note to themselves to let them know not to go to a particular planet. Here we see they had enough sense to follow that advice, but we still end up meeting the Aschen though. '2001' shows us the alternate way of contact, where we met them via the third planet. I loved the way in which we were dealing with future knowledge wrapped in a cryptic package. I also loved that invention of Brad's — creating an entire world, as well as a whole new time. It's then we find out that Ronny Cox's character finally becomes President — that was kinda neat. And it was so cool that in this world, the *Stargate* has become the standard mode of transportation!"

The biggest thrill for the director was the discovery of one of the most elusive secrets in the universe: "We think we found out what the Technician's name is. When someone calls him Walter and the Technician confirms that that might be his name, it could be a bit of a red herring, because in fact — his name is Norman!" Labouring under the illusion that the world needs to know this, DeLuise reveals, "OK, it's actually Norman Walter. The Technician's name is Norman Walter. We know that his last name is Davis from his patch, right? So put it all together, and you have his full name. We thought it would be funny to call him something, you know, nerdy. Not that Norman and Walters are nerds, but as far as we are concerned, that's his name. Some people are named Billy Jo or Billy Jack. His name is Norman Walter." So glad we got that sorted out. ⋏

Desperate Measures

Written by: Joseph Mallozzi and Paul Mullie
Directed by: Bill Gereghty

Guest cast: John de Lancie (Colonel Frank Simmons), Tom McBeath (Colonel Harry Maybourne), Bill Marchant (Adrian Conrad), Andrew Johnston (Doctor), Ted Cole (Doctor), Carrie Genzei (Diana Mendez)

Carter is kidnapped by a bunch of MiBs and taken to a centre specialising in secret experiments. There's shades of aliens being abducted, rather than alien abductions, when it transpires that Colonel Maybourne has sold a larval Goa'uld to an extremely rich and powerful individual, who wants to cure his terminal illness by becoming a host. Too bright to just 'open mouth and insert snake', the slippery customer first wants to find out how Carter managed to survive Jolinar's implant. O'Neill and Maybourne team up to track down Carter and the Goa'uld, unaware that the even slimier Colonel Simmons is working against their every move. It's more a case of a shot in the back rather than a stab in the back, but... whodunnit?

Daniel

> "I think I just electrocuted myself."

Writers Joe Mallozzi and Paul Mullie are huge fans of the conspiracy storylines. Says Mullie, "I've said it in every interview, but I'll say it again: what I like, as a fan of *Stargate*, is variety. You can have a big arc-driven System Lord story; we can do a one-off comedic escapade. We also really need to have an NID facet. When we did 'Desperate Measures', it wasn't really a full-on conspiracy plotline; that was kind of the 'C' story. The episode is somewhat similar to 'Chain Reaction', in that we are looking into shady dealing of the NID." Joe Mallozzi continues, "Colonel Maybourne is fast becoming one of our favourite characters to write for. He's such a good bad guy. I mean, it's not like he's a Goa'uld, or has no redeeming qualities."

Actor Tom McBeath — who certainly isn't a bad guy — has a touch of amnesia when it comes to this episode. "I really don't remember that much about the show, other than I thought the writers did a pretty fine job," he volunteers. "Plus I recall Richard sort of changed things on the fly in our scenes. I enjoy that. I love the dynamic we have together. We filmed part of 'Desperate Measures' in an old hospital for the mentally handicapped," McBeath continues. "It was full of ghosts, and was just a horrible place to be. The *Stargate*

*Above: One slick, sick
individual.*

art department did a fantastic job with lots of on-set construction work, but even so, the place was probably built in the 1930s and at one time was presumably full of desperately unhappy people. There were stairways in this building with cages that were built to hold these people. It was really scary. I didn't see any ghosts, but you certainly got a very creepy feeling. In fact, I wasn't very well when we were shooting this episode — but it wasn't all down to the bad vibes." Keeping a very straight face, but with a distinct twinkle in his eye McBeath goes on, "Actually, I did have some sort of stomach disorder I'd picked up. We were just ready to roll, and I had to say to the director — 'I have to go vomit.' He thought I was just kidding, but I went 'Oh no! I really do have to do it.' There you go — that's a little bit of colour for the book." Er, thanks Mr McBeath… ʌ

Wormhole X-Treme!

Written by: Brad Wright, Joseph Mallozzi and Paul Mullie **Teleplay by:** Joseph Mallozzi and Paul Mullie **Directed by:** Peter DeLuise	**Guest cast:** Willie Garson (Martin Lloyd), Michael DeLuise (Nick Marlowe/Colonel Danning), Peter DeLuise (Director), Jill Teed (Yolanda Reese/Stacy Munroe), Robert Lewis (Dr Peter Tanner), Benjamin Ratner (Producer), Christian Bocher (Raymond Gunne/Dr Levant)

S G-1 are reunited with Marty the alien (last seen in 'Point of No Return', in season four). He now has no recollection of his other-worldly origins, but is working as a consultant on a new TV show, which has a premise that owes rather a lot to the Stargate project. O'Neill is sent to the *Wormhole X-Treme!* set, under the guise of special military adviser to the show, to find out what is going on. Meanwhile, an alien ship has been detected *en route* to Earth, trying to connect with the pod Marty rediscovered on his previous encounter with SG-1. The race is on to uncover the truth, find out what the aliens want and work out why Marty no longer claims to be an alien — and all before the TV show hits the top of the ratings!

Dr Levant

"Just because they're aliens and their skulls are transparent doesn't meant they don't have rights."

It's a touch of the 'ET phones home' for this special 100th episode. Peter DeLuise was thrilled to be given a 'big comedy' to direct and says, "We tried to give the audience all the inside scoops that we could. If you watch the background, you'll see tons and tons of visual gags and in jokes. For example, Death Gliders being carried through the background; Thor, the puppet, being defibrillated — cool stuff like that." The director insists that a bit of poetic licence was taken with his own character. "As for the Pyrotechnics light show — I don't usually scream 'bigger, bigger, bigger!'," he insists, "but I do end up saying, in a calm, rational voice, 'This should be big. It should be fiery.'" Eventually he admits, "OK, it's Martin Wood's and my job to make things look big, so it's not *totally* unheard of for me to scream 'bigger, bigger, bigger!'" One confession out of the way, he goes on, "The backlot in the episode is the real backlot at Bridge studios. That's how it looks to us every day, except for that amount of colour, which some may argue looked like Walt Disney threw up. Actually, it's not usually that colourful *and* there aren't usually that

many busty background characters hanging around. But the real crew were in as many of the scenes as possible.

"Now granted, the plot was pretty damn thin," the director continues, "but it was a great excuse to be in that environment. I just loved all the various things we slipped in. You can watch it many times, and see all sorts of stuff you haven't noticed before."

So what's DeLuise's favourite 'Easter Egg' (to use the DVD term for hidden surprises) to look for in the episode? "The big crane shot at the end," he says. "That's our entire crew, the real one, onscreen right there. If you look really carefully, you can see the real O'Neill, and the photo double O'Neill. In the deep, deep background after the aliens go away in their ship, you can see that O'Neill and Teal'c are in the trucks almost at the top of the frame. But that is not really Richard Dean Anderson. That is, in fact, Bill Nicholai, his photo double. Richard is down towards the lower right portion of the frame in his civilian clothes, taking pictures!" λ

Above: Four intrepid souls taking wormhole travel to extremes.

Proving Ground

Written by: Ron Wilkerson	Guest cast: Courtney J. Stevens (Lt Elliot), Elisabeth
Directed by: Andy Mikita	Rosen (Jennifer Hailey), Grace Park (Satterfield), David
	Kopp (Grogan), Michael Kopsa (General Kerrigan)

t's a case of bluff and double bluff when some academy graduates are put through their paces in preparation for joining the elite at the SGC. A particularly promising group, which includes Cadet Hailey (first seen in season four's 'Prodigy'), get to shadow SG-1. Coming under the auspices of Colonel O'Neill, the group appears to be failing miserably. When an unexpected 'foothold' situation occurs, it seems that Daniel Jackson has turned to the dark side, and O'Neill has been injured. The rookies are left to deal with this critical state of affairs on their own...

Carter to O'Neill

"Think back to when you were their age."

"I was never their age."

"The episode centred round us testing the new recruits," begins Amanda Tapping, "and it was quite funny because we just kept going from bluff to double bluff. It was like, 'Well, we have a foothold situation' and then, 'Naw! We were just kidding.' 'No Wait! We *do* have a foothold situation.' 'No, we don't!'" This episode proved to be quite the training ground for more than just the characters. Amanda Tapping found herself giving helpful hints throughout filming.

"Elizabeth Rosen and Courtney Stevens did a fantastic job," Tapping continues. "Courtney was really great, he was so intuitive and so sweet, and we were lucky to get him back for another episode later in the year. However, with this one, what I remember most about shooting was that I was like a mother hen. I felt incredibly *old* around these young cast members! I suddenly realised — I was around their age when I started doing this show. So I found myself giving them some hints, and kept reminding them of stuff because they would often forget things that are now second nature to Richard Dean Anderson, Christopher and the rest of our guys. For instance, how to carry your gun! Now our armourer is phenomenal, he has all the technical expertise and does a great job of imparting that knowledge, but there was this one scene where I am about to go into my lab, and just before the blast doors open, I'm looking at the newbies — and they weren't flagging their triggers with their index fingers." Wise to

the fact that not that many of us have a clue what she's on about, Tapping explains, "You have to have your index finger straight next to the trigger of a gun, rather than curled around it, so that you don't just fire off accidentally. So, I'm looking at our new cast and some of them actually have their fingers on the trigger. I'm standing off-camera going, 'Flag your fingers, flag your fingers!' in a not very subtle stage whisper. They were all looking at me going, 'What???' and I'm going, 'Never, ever have your fingers round the trigger. Look professional you guys, come on!'

"There was another scene where one of the newbies was holding his gun up ready, and I had to pass in front of him, but he kept it there. I just looked at him as if to say, 'What are you going to do? Shoot me? This is where your so-called 'friendly fire' comes into play, soldier! You lower your weapon when a friend walks past, and then bring it back up ready against the enemy.'" Laughing at her own zeal Tapping admits, "I was getting stuck right in there! I was a little like a drill sergeant. I remember thinking to myself, 'Wow! You are taking this just a *bit* too seriously.'" ⋋

Above: O'Neill has a quiet word with the new recruits.

48 Hours

Written by: Robert C. Cooper	Guest cast: David Hewlett (Dr McKay), John de Lancie
Directed by: Peter Woeste	(Colonel Frank Simmons), Tom McBeath (Colonel Harry
	Marbourne), Colin Cunningham (Major Davis), Bill
	Marchant (Goa'uld within Adrian Conrad), Garry Chalk
	(Russian Colonel), Gary Jones (Sgt Davis)

t's even more hectic than usual at the SGC, in a race against time to save Teal'c, track down a rogue Goa'uld and outwit a government scientist — all within a forty-eight-hour time frame. SG-1 are staging a tactical retreat (whilst getting their butts kicked by an army of Jaffa), but Teal'c delays his jump through the Gate to blow up Tanith's ship. The vessel crashes into the Gate just as Teal'c enters the wormhole. The resulting damage leaves Teal'c's essence floating in the ether. Hampered by a cocky government scientist (the world expert seemingly, though he's never seen a Stargate), Major Carter tries to work out a way to get Teal'c back. Daniel and Major Davis go cap in hand to sweet talk the Russians into volunteering their Gate, whilst O'Neill and Maybourne join forces again to rout out a Goa'uld in the hope that he could provide a way to release Teal'c.

McKay to Carter

"I always had a real weakness for dumb blondes."

"Go suck a lemon."

"I still like the original title, 'Teal'c Interrupted', better," insists Robert Cooper. "Believe it or not, this show started as a notion I got remembering an old episode of *M*A*S*H* where Hawkeye was trying desperately to get something — an incubator of some kind I think. He had to continually trade one thing for another to finally get the thing he wanted. The whole thing went round and round. In that spirit, I wanted the team to have to face one obstacle after another before they are able to get one of their team members back.

"It actually turned into something very different to the *M*A*S*H* episode in the end," Cooper admits, "with three completely separate yet intertwined storylines, with Jack, Sam and Daniel working toward the necessary elements they needed to get Teal'c out of the Gate. I also loved David Hewlett's performance so much, I wrote him a bigger part in 'Redemption'. By the way, the joke about McKay being allergic to lemons is a good-natured dig at a former writer on the show!

"I also thought we hadn't done a story that focused on the downright

incredible-ness of the Stargate in a while," Cooper points out. "Since it's our franchise, we should remind people every now and then just how damn incredible it is, and how far out of our element we are when we try and use it!"

Above: Teal'c prepares to dispatch Tanith.

Cooper also offers a touch of insider gossip: "One last interesting tidbit is the death of Tanith. We never intended to kill his character this way. We would have much preferred to have him face off with Teal'c in a grand showdown, but the actor was holding us up and frankly we just couldn't afford to give him what he wanted. So the Tanith in the cockpit of the Alkesh is actually a computer generated effect!" ⋏

Summit

Written by: Joseph Mallozzi and Paul Mullie Directed by: Martin Wood	Guest cast: Carmen Argenziano (Carter/Selmak), Anna-Louise Plowman (Osiris), Cliff Simon (Ba'al), Courtney J. Stevens (Lt Elliot), Jennifer Calvert (Ren'al), William de Vry (Aldwin), Anthony Ulc (Major Mansfield), Vince Crestejo (Yu the Great)

The best laid plans of men and Goa'uld go slightly awry when SG-1, in cahoots with the Tok'ra, embark on a bold plan to wipe out a shipload of System Lords. It seems that one powerful Goa'uld is refusing to play nice, and is attacking all the other System Lords. Naturally they all band together to decide what can be done with the interloper. Daniel Jackson agrees to go undercover as Yu's slave in order to gather intelligence and more importantly, deliver a poison which can kill all the Goa'uld present within seconds.

However, the arrival of the lovely but deadly Osiris surprises Daniel and temporarily thwarts his plans...

Daniel

"It's kinda like Goa'uld Mardi Gras here."

Director Martin Woods finds that "the interesting thing about 'Summit' and 'Last Stand' is that they are two completely different stories, but most people don't think about that because there is a connection. The episodes are actually two different stories, intercut really nicely." One of the highlights for Wood was the introduction of a whole bunch of new System Lords: "I liked that we got to bring in a new lot of System Lords, but the problem was that they weren't all actors with actual dialogue. Some of them were played by extras, because the characters didn't have proper lines. They were just sitting there, nodding sagely, but we were fighting to get these people to actually have something to say. The ironic thing is that two of them *did* have lines, but they were cut out! The only two who ended up having lines were Ba'al and Olokum. Oh, and you get Bastet talking a little bit, but otherwise... zip. There was a lot of stuff cut out of 'Summit' in the end. We were eleven minutes over and it ended up being quite difficult shuffling stuff back and forth."

Needless to say, Wood enjoyed working with all the System Lords — but he has a soft spot for Ba'al: "Of course, we all love Ba'al and had such a good time with him. Cliff Simon has been back a number

of times because he had a classic villain look. If he had a handlebar moustache he'd be twirling it all the time!" Co-producer and writer Joe Mallozzi was so impressed with the suave System Lord that he 'borrowed' Ba'al's costume from designer Christina's McQuarrie's store to wear at the Gatecon convention in 2002! Lord of all he surveyed, the resplendent Ba'al Mallozzi delighted the crowds with his description of the souvlaki that could be found in an eaterie close by the convention hotel. Apparently frequented by the Goa'uld, the establishment is aptly called Cronus restaurant.

Martin Wood has nothing but praise for the sartorial elegance of the rest of the deities: "'Summit' looked absolutely gorgeous. We had that beautiful set that allowed us to do that 'walk around' shot, where we introduced everybody. Christine McQuarrie really did us proud with those wonderful costumes that, appropriately enough, looked divine. However, Michael Shanks hated his arm bands. He thought they looked like water wings. I thought they looked great, but then again, I wasn't the one who had to wear them!" Λ

Above: A gallery of rogues.

Last Stand

Written by: Robert C. Cooper	Guest cast: Carmen Argenziano (Jacob/Selmak),
Directed by: Martin Wood	Anna-Louise Plowman (Osiris), Cliff Simon (Ba'al),
	Courtney J. Stevens (Lt Elliot), Jennifer Calvert
	(Ren'al), William de Vry (Aldwin), Anthony Ulc (Major
	Mansfield), Vince Crestejo (Yu the Great)

acob Carter manages to convince a skeptical Daniel that his ex-girlfriend Sarah can no longer be saved, now that her body is inhabited by the Goa'uld Osiris. Brought to his senses, Daniel injects her with a mind-altering drug so that she believes him to be Yu's slave. Returning to the war council, Daniel discovers that Osiris is actually working on behalf of Lord Anubis, and realises that by keeping to the programme he will actually help rather than hinder the bad guy. Things go from bad to worse when he also hears that Zipacna knows the location of the Tok'ra base, and has sent minions to destroy it…

Daniel

"You'd think a race advanced enough to fly around in space ships would be smart enough to have seatbelts."

Speaking of the connection between this and the previous episode Martin Wood states, "It was good to bring back Osiris: I loved the whole scene between her and Daniel where she walks in and just drawls, 'Daniel Jackson.' The changeover point was really interesting for me as director, because I felt that when we went from 'Summit' to 'Last Stand', we had to have her walking in and speaking to Daniel. I didn't want them to do the, 'Previously on *Stargate SG-1*… and now…' voiceover, because I wanted to see the door closing and then the uninterrupted continuation."

Other than the costumes, the System Lords, the very cool set and the pleasing fact that there were two different worlds involved in this story, neither of which was Earth, what *really* impressed Wood were the visual effects. "We were in Tok'ra tunnels and there were huge explosions going on," he recalls. "James Tichenor does the most amazing things with basically a flint and some bearskin. He really does! He has barely enough budget, but manages to put movie quality effects on the small screen. He's nothing less than a genius.

"Next time you watch, just look at that whole scene with the crashing cargo ship. I read that sequence, and began wondering how we were going to do it. Robert Cooper walked in and said, in no uncertain terms, 'This is how I want it.' James and I were delighted, but looked at each

Above: Daniel sees to the petty needs of Yu.

other and went, 'It's going to be *very* expensive.' And Robert said, 'I don't care!' So we both rubbed our hands with glee and said, 'Fine!' You get so conditioned to *not* getting that response in episodic television. Having been given our head, we really went for it. One of my very favourite shots is when you see this glider going down, and cutting the trees. We shot it as a model, with blades on the wings. The model was actually strung on wire in the parking lot of the studios. I really, really loved that sequence because we also saw the inside of the cargo ship, which we shot by shaking the hell out of the camera! The end result would not have been so spectacular without Robert Cooper supporting us and pushing for that scene."

Sadly one of the Tok'ra was less than elated to find that she was going to crash and burn in the episode. "Council woman Ren'al, aka Jennifer Calvert, knew the show very well, and when she walked on set at the beginning of the morning she goes, 'This is the lab, right?... And where is the sarcophagus? There has to be a sarcophagus.'" Wood recalls. "When we were rehearsing the death scene it was just hilarious listening to her English accent and her plaintive cries of 'Is there a sarcophagus nearby?'" ⅄

Fail Safe

Story by: Joseph Mallozzi and Paul Mullie
Directed by: Andy Mikita

Guest cast: Colin Cunningham (Major Davis), Gary Jones (Sgt Davis), David Bloom (Spellman), Greg Anderson (Webber), Michael Teigen (Telescope Guy), Kristen Williamson (Jalen)

SG-1 find themselves up against something even larger than your average Goa'uld when a giant asteroid is discovered hurtling towards Earth. They are sent to try to deflect the rock from its current trajectory, thus saving the planet yet again. However, the asteroid is in fact part of a huge plot by the Goa'uld, who have pumped it full of Naquadah so they can destroy the Earth without breaking the Asgard protected planet treaty. Can our boys and girls save us? It's time to suit up…

O'Neill

"Carter, I can see my house."

Writer Joe Mallozzi starts off by saying, "Every so often the fans will complain, 'This script is junk' or 'This writer writes terrible scripts', but what some people don't realise is that we *all* have a hand in the scripts." Writing partner Paul Mullie butts in with, "Pay no attention. Joe is trying to weasel out of any responsibility for ripping off *Armaggeddon*." Obviously teasing his partner, Mullie goes on, "My idea is that *Armaggeddon* wasn't a particularly original idea in the first place. The idea of a giant asteroid crashing into Earth, and what we would do about it, is a very old science fiction idea.

"What I always like to do when we do sci-fi stories that resemble films, or episodes of other shows, is to put the special *Stargate* spin on it, that little *Stargate* fourth act twist. In this case, it was the discovery that the asteroid was almost entirely made out of Naquadah. At first we thought we could just stick a nuclear bomb in it (that's what they always do in the movies), but then we realise — wait a minute, if we do that the result will be ten times worse!"

Mullie also reveals that the episode was particularly hard to write: "The real problem was thinking through the visual effects. Planning them for screen direction was a nightmare. We had to think of where the asteroid was in relation to Earth, and marry that to where the Earth was in relation to the ship, *and* where the ship was in relation to the asteroid! If the ship is going left to right, but the asteroid is

spinning, then the Earth should rise in a particular direction. But in space there is no neutral, everything is dependent on where you're looking. So what's technically correct can often seem like a mistake to the audience. Sometimes you have to make a choice as to what is technically right, as opposed to what looks right, and vice versa.

Above: In space, no one can hear you screaming to get out of a spacesuit.

"This was one of those episodes where Joe was just rolling his eyes, while Brad Wright and I were being two geeks having these long, involved discussions about the technicalities!"

The part that did amuse rather than frustrate Mr Mallozzi was the strange case of the spacesuits: "We see Teal'c and O'Neill in spacesuits, coming to rescue Carter and Jackson. They realise that Sam and Daniel are sealed in the escape pods, and have to bring the atmosphere back up in the ship — which they go about doing. What you will notice in the episode is that they aren't wearing their space-suits when they do actually release their comrades. These suits take an hour to put on, and presumably take an hour to take off, so we can only assume that rather than release them right away, Teal'c and O'Neill took an hour to remove their suits before releasing their friends!" Mullie concludes, "Knowing O'Neill's sense of humour, I can't argue with his logic. I would have done the same thing." ⅄

The Warrior

Written by: Christopher Judge
Teleplay by: Peter DeLuise
Directed by: Peter DeLuise

Guest cast: Tony Amendola (Bra'tac), Rick Worthy (K'tano), Obi Ndefo (Rak'nor), Kirby Morrow (Tara'c), Vince Crestejo (Yu the Great)

B ra'tac and Teal'c believe themselves to be in good company when they encounter a charismatic Jaffa leader called K'tano, who has rallied a large group of Jaffa against the Goa'uld. Believing this man to be a potential ally, SG-1 go to his base with weapons, food and medicines. O'Neill becomes suspicious when he hears that K'tano teaches the art of surrender rather than survival, and sends hundreds of people on suicide missions. Voicing his suspicions causes a rift between him and Teal'c, until it's discovered that the leader is not all he appears to be — and is in fact a Goa'uld masquerading as Jaffa. The exposed Imoteph finds that Hell hath no fury like a ticked-off Teal'c...

O'Neill

"Hey, you in the skirt... get that target swinging a little."

Peter DeLuise informs us that "Chris Judge came up with the idea of using Imoteph, who was kind of the da Vinci of the Egyptians. He was heavily into architecture and medical advancements, and after his death was deified in Egyptian mythology. We thought he'd be a good guy to look at, and we came up with a new slant on the way in which System Lords could get followers. We made it so this undercover fella was claiming to be his own First Prime. He 'killed' himself by staging his own death, and then rallied the troops and did a Teal'c/Bra'tac thing by saying, 'Follow me. The gods are false. Follow me and I will lead you to victory.' He was never a very powerful System Lord, so he thought this was a good way of getting some Jaffa to swell the ranks of his own army.

"So Imoteph pulls the wool over our eyes, and makes us believe that he's collected a whole bunch of rebel Jaffa," DeLuise continues. "We find out about his alliance with Yu, and also that he was intending to doublecross him. Yu, being a clever guy, had anticipated this move and sent Teal'c right back to assassinate Imoteph. Teal'c gets so upset that Imoteph would deceive the Jaffa because this is like the ultimate insult — using the Jaffa hatred of the Goa'uld to solicit support, whilst being a Goa'uld yourself! So they have a big knock down, drag out fight.

Above: Master Bra'tac demonstrates the correct use of a staff.

"That was the first episode where we used a special camera rig that I invented. I drew some specs for the rig on a piece of paper, and the special effects guys were able to make it," DeLuise explains. "We call it the Revolva. We used it on the *Matrix*-style shot where we were going round and round the actors — I was very pleased with the results we got."

"My memories of 'The Warrior'," says Tony Amendola, "are of those wonderful South American martial arts. I also remember Peter DeLuise's energy during the shoot. Peter's ability to energise people — when he is trying to control a crowd of a hundred, and get exactly what he wants from everybody — is a wonder to behold. Sometimes he does it with a steady stream of profanity, which is hilarious. It's not offensive, and gets everybody pumped up and laughing because of what he's saying and how he's saying it." On a more serious note, Amendola shares, "I found the false messiah aspect of the story really, really interesting. Then came the realisation at the end where we say, 'You know what? We have to do it ourselves.' Ultimately, what it comes down to is the knowledge that you can't look outside yourself for answers. You really have to reach inside yourself." λ

Menace

Written by: James Tichenor	Guest cast: Danielle Nicolet (Reese), Colin Lawrence
Teleplay by: Peter DeLuise	(Major Warren), Tracy Westerholm (SF), Kski Gugushe
Directed by: Martin Wood	(SF), Kyle Riefsnyder (SF), Dan Shea (Sgt Siler)

When SG-1 encounter a young girl abandoned on a deserted planet, further investigations uncover the fact that she is an android, with no memory of being manufactured. Daniel befriends the emotionally immature girl who presents him with a 'toy' in gratitude. Unfortunately, it's a gift that keeps on giving — with deadly results. Reese has been making Replicators which, true to form, have destroyed the planet. Unable to deal with the magnitude of her mistake, the android goes quietly mad. Meanwhile, the Replicators attack and SG-1 must figure out a way to stop the 'toys' before they destroy their toy box.

Daniel to O'Neill

"It has a heart beat?"

"It has a heart?"

'Menace' was visual effects supervisor James Tichenor's first episode as a story writer for *Stargate SG-1*. "Basically what happened was, I pitched a story were we go to a world and find a woman who has creatures she can control," he recalls. "As the story progresses, we realise that she is actually an android, who uses these creatures as a defence mechanism. It's sort of a *Forbidden Planet*-type of thing. I'd pitched a couple of ideas in the past, but they had been laughed off (as well they should!). But this one caught the producers' interest. They thought, 'Hey… what if we make her the person who created the Replicators?' So they bought the idea from me, and had me write an outline. Peter DeLuise then wrote a script, which Rob Cooper then re-wrote. The essence of my story is still there though. It all came from the idea that good people do bad things. I wanted to show that Reese, the creator of the Replicators, wasn't evil — just scared."

The ever-modest Peter DeLuise begins by applauding colleague James Tichenor for the original idea. "Plus," he says, "I do have to give James extra credit, because he was branching out from straight VFX to the next level. That is very cool.

"It was also cool," DeLuise continues, "that Reese, this inventor who herself is an invention, is able to manipulate nanobots — and with that technology she can re-order matter. In so doing, she created Replicators. But they have an imperfect program — an imperfect

directive to replicate, because they don't have a higher structure of meaning. Eventually, in 'Unnatural Selection' they evolve into something more human-like."

Michael Shanks enjoyed playing with Reese's new toys: "This was a fun episode. We got to touch on the Replicators storyline, but 'Menace' also had a great emotional arc, coupled with the part of the mythology that deals with the origins of the Replicator technology. I guess the emotional stuff, mixed with the mythology, mixed with the origins of that particular 'villain' meant there was something for everybody! Personally, I enjoyed the little bit of Jack/Daniel tension and whatnot. That was a highlight."

Shanks also reveals that the episode could have turned out to be quite a family affair. "My girlfriend Lexa Doig was originally asked if she would like to play the part of Reese, but she had commitments to *Andromeda* and couldn't do it. I think there was also the issue that she would have been playing an android again (like she does on *Andromeda*). That might have been something that scared her away a little bit too. But working with Danielle was great. She's got a lot of 'chops', as we say in the acting world, and she did a wonderful job." ⋏

Above: Carter and O'Neill are less than thrilled with Reese's toys.

The Sentinel

Written by: Ron Wilkerson **Directed by:** Peter DeLuise	**Guest cast:** Henry Gibson (Marul), Frank Cassini (Colonel Sean Grieves), Christina Cox (Lt Kershaw), David Kopp (Lt Grogan), Gary Jones (Sgt Davis)

The dastardly Goa'uld are at it again, trying to barge in and take over a planet, but the indigenous inhabitants believe their super-shield Sentinel device will protect them. Unfortunately, the nerds at the NID have been up to their dirty tricks, and scuppered said device. Things look bleak until SG-1 enlist the help of two convicted criminals…

Kershaw to Daniel

"I feel better just knowing there's an archaeologist watching our backs..."

"... which end do the bullets go in again?"

A major highlight for the director of 'The Sentinel' was being in the presence of one of his heroes, a comic actor of the old school: "I got to work with Henry Gibson, who is wonderful." In his own inimitable way, DeLuise describes the progression of the episode: "We allude to the fact that Zipacna is trying to take over this planet, and ultimately kill everyone. Originally, Zipacna was just an extra. He was walking down the hallway in 'Summit', but he's become part of System Lord lore now! So, he was in orbit around this planet, and was requiring them to kow-tow to him — but he got his ass kicked by the Sentinel device.

"The original idea was to go and get some of our old bad guys to help us with this new mission. It was going to be the 'Dirty Dozen', but it turned out to be the 'Dirty Duo'. So we had these two characters which we *implied* were in the episode 'Shades of Grey' (back in season three), in the crowd of personnel operating for the NID out of the off-world base. Brad Wright did a clever thing. In the 'Previously on *Stargate…*' bit at the beginning of 'The Sentinel', he included a scene from 'Shades of Grey', but added in new shots of Grieves and Kershaw that we had in fact not seen 'previously' at all! He made you *think* they were in that other episode, but they definitely were not. They were new characters that we'd never seen before." Sneakiness worthy of the Goa'uld!

Indulging his passion for dirty things, DeLuise jokes that "we wanted someone very dirty to play these bad guys, so we went for Frank Cassini, who is very dirty, and a girl named Christina Cox, who doesn't look that dirty on the outside but is dirty on the inside. She's a dirty girl, as they say!"

Uncharacteristically serious for a time, DeLuise confesses that 'The Sentinel' will always stay in his memory because of the tragic events that unfolded during filming. "It was a challenge, because we were working on that show when 9/11 happened. So it was particularly difficult to be working. Everybody on set had their televisions on, and it was very hard to concentrate because of what was happening. We thought the whole world as we knew it was over, and here we were doing this silly sci-fi television show. A lot of film crews did stop filming, but we had been at work for a while and we decided that whoever was at fault, whoever was trying to screw us up, did it because they wanted things to stop. It was what they wanted. However, we decided we weren't gonna do that. We were going to carry on working, as a way of saying, 'You didn't get to us.' We did that as a mark of respect for the people who died, and the families whose lives had to carry on. For me, it was very difficult to ask, 'Could you stand on this mark and say this line?' knowing that those buildings were crashing down and people were dying. It was one of the tougher days I've ever had." ⋏

Above: *Gentle Marul, manhandled by menaces.*

Meridian

Story by: Robert C. Cooper	Guest cast: Corin Nemec (Jonas Quinn), Carmen
Directed by: Will Waring	Argenziano (Jacob/Selmak), Gary Jones (Sgt Davis),
	Mel Harris (Oma Desala), Dave Hurtubise (Tomis Leed),
	Kevin McCrae (Scientist)

D aniel appears through the Stargate suffering from high degree burns and a lethal dose of radiation. As Daniel steadily loses his battle against the poisoning, O'Neill tries to unravel the mysterious claim that his friend deliberately sabotaged an experiment on another planet. O'Neill appeals to their ambassador, Jonas Quinn, to reveal the truth and restore Daniel's good name. Meanwhile another battle is being waged, as Daniel has to decide whether to return to this mortal coil or give it up to join the ranks of the Ascended, thereby continuing his spiritual journey. Naturally he turns to Jack to help him make that decision.

O'Neill to Daniel

"I may have grown to admire you... a little... I think."

It's unlikely there's ever been a bigger ruckus over the demise of a character than the fuss created when Daniel Jackson hung up his hat and went off to investigate higher things. From the moment spoilers were posted on the Internet, enraged (and on occasion deranged) fans blasted the producers, the entire writing team, the suits at MGM and even the cast as having driven "poor Michael" out of the show. Several websites, including one created by the 'Save Daniel Jackson' campaign vented all sorts of spleen and bile against the makers of the show. Some fans collected enough money to place an ad in a prominent Hollywood paper to show their solidarity for Michael Shanks. Though claiming victory for getting Shanks back in season seven, the truth of the matter is that their highly vocal objections, coupled with the equally strong opinions of 'the other side', simply underlined the massive amount of interest in the show. It's something which the SCI FI Channel had no doubt taken into account when they happily invited the *Stargate SG-1* crew to jump through the portal for another season.

Understandably, things were a trifle gloomy on set during the actual filming of the episode. Teryl Rothery admits, "I was a wreck. I had some scenes where I just couldn't stop crying. I know that as a doctor, I was meant to be able to contain my feelings and conduct myself in an appropriately professional manner, but every time I

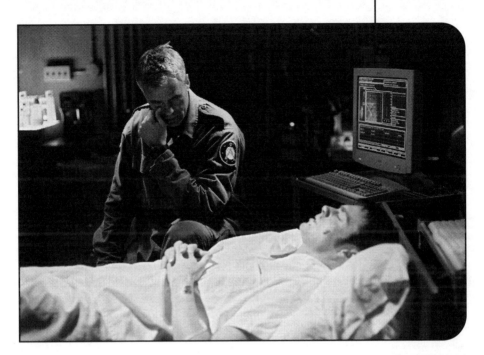

Above: O'Neill finally admits his feelings for Daniel Jackson.

thought of Daniel's pain and suffering, my heart would fill and the tears would flow. Of course, it was ten times worse knowing that we really were saying *au revoir* to Michael too."

"I take my hat off to Corin Nemec, though," says Don S. Davis. "We welcomed him on board, and he was respectful of the emotion which encompassed us at that time. He went positively and quietly about his business like the gentleman he is."

"I think that episode might stick in my memory!" Michael Shanks jokes. "Something happens to Daniel, and he packs his bags and moves on from where he was at that time in the series. He's no longer a regular character. That was kind of emotional. Everybody was saying goodbye to an everyday thing. I mean, these people become your family, and the ramifications of that never really dawn on you till afterwards. But I think I realised that what we had was coming to an end. There was a lot of emotional stuff on set, and it was difficult. I think the episode turned out well, considering the different agendas that were met. So, there's no discontent there, but what kind of closure can you achieve in any one episode? When all's said and done though, I think that for what it was meant to do, 'Meridian' was more than adequate, and serviced my character well." ⋏

Revelations

Written by: Joseph Mallozzi and Paul Mullie
Directed by: Martin Wood

Guest cast: Anna Louise Plowman (Osiris), Teryl Rothery (Heimdall), David Palffy (Anubis)

Life is a touch gloomy at the SGC without Daniel Jackson. SG-1 try to struggle on as normal, but things obviously are not the same. Their minds become re-focussed when they receive a visit from Freyr, an Asgard buddy of Thor's who tells the team that not only is their planet in danger from the Replicators, but that Anubis has surrounded their planet and Thor has been taken prisoner and is presumed dead. The gang head off on a rescue mission and meet up with Heimdall, an Asgard scientist of the highest order. Together they find Thor alive, if not well, on Osiris's ship. O'Neill and Teal'c attempt to rescue the little guy whilst Carter assists Heimdall to evacuate the contents of his lab, as much of the information he's amassed could help save his race from extinction.

Carter

"We were a team, Teal'c."

Amanda Tapping feels that this episode finally started to show how close Carter had come to all her team mates: "There's always been a sense of deep affection between Carter and O'Neill, but Chris Judge and I had been pushing for us to also see some tangible manifestation of Carter and Teal'c's relationship. We wanted to see some solidification of their friendship. I think we took some more steps towards that in 'Revelations', but we still have a long way to go." Never mind Carter being close to Teal'c, it's evident just how close Tapping has become to Carter, as the actress describes her approach to the episode: "Carter, O'Neill and Teal'c are still grieving the loss of Daniel Jackson. The way I play it is that my character has this need not only to talk about the loss of a very important person in our lives, but to acknowledge that we do feel this way and are having a hard time dealing with our feelings. It seemed to me that Teal'c and O'Neill were just a little too pragmatic. At first, I didn't think our concern came across that well, but having watched the episode again, there is a sense that the characters have their own private moments of grief over our loss of Daniel — but we do have to move on with our lives."

"Carter is the first member of SG-1 to warm up to Jonas," comments Corin Nemec. "I think her natural compassion coupled with her natural

Above: Osiris shows her displeasure at being thwarted by Thor.

sense of curiosity, which is something she has in common with Jonas, helps that along. Jonas and Teal'c do end up bonding, although it takes some time, because they are both aliens who left their homes under somewhat of a cloud, and who find themselves trying to assimilate into a world vastly different from their own. Teal'c has had years to do this, so I think he appreciates and understands the difficulties Jonas will face. Colonel O'Neill is a different kettle of fish altogether. He's a hard nut to crack, but Jonas is extremely easy going and is eager to make friends with this guy. He knows there are a few trust issues and a touch of resentment there, but I think Jonas may yet win him over."

Richard Dean Anderson came under fire from some of the die-hard Daniel-ites after his comments about choosing to treat the archaeologist's demise in characteristically pragmatic terms. "But Jack O'Neill is a seasoned soldier," Anderson reasons. "He's seen action and has lost comrades. I think at this point in his life, it's reasonable to assume that he would take the time to grieve privately, but publicly he still has a job to do." ⋏

REDEMPTION [PART 1]

Written by: Robert C. Cooper Directed by: Martin Wood	Guest cast: Tony Amendola (Bra'tac), Christopher Kennedy (Dr Larry Murphy), David Hewlett (Dr McKay), Garry Chalk (Colonel Chekov), Neil Denis (Rya'c), Gary Jones (Sgt Davis), Tobias Mehler (Lt Simmons), David Palffy (Anubis)

I t's three months after Daniel Jackson's departure, and tension is running high at Stargate Command, as SG-1 struggle to find an acceptable replacement. Jonas Quinn is unable to gain full acceptance in his new surroundings, but the Naquadria he brought with him from his home planet has enabled the scientists at Area 51 to create the X-302, the first human-built spacecraft capable of interstellar travel. Teal'c goes off-world to respond to a family crisis and, with the help of Master Bra'tac, is finally reconciled with his son. When the safety of Earth is threatened by Anubis's new energy weapon, O'Neill and Carter attempt to use the X-302 to contact the Asgard for assistance. Alerted to the danger facing his friends' home planet, Teal'c formulates a plan to destroy the weapon at its source.

"'Redemption' was not originally a two-parter," Robert Cooper begins, "but the script was too long, and then I found a huge hole in the story as I was writing. I called Brad and said, 'Hey, I might have a two-parter here.' I've always wanted to do more with Teal'c and his son, but never had the story to fit those scenes into. Now I needed a B-story, where someone went off to destroy the device with which Anubis was destroying us from afar. We also introduced the X-302, a

Anubis

A funerary deity of Ancient Egypt, his name is derived from the word meaning 'to putrefy'. Known as Lord of the Dead, it was thought that Anubis held the scales on which a person's worth is judged at their death. If the heart was lighter than a feather, he led the soul to heaven. If not, the soul was destroyed. In the *Stargate* universe, Anubis is part Goa'uld, part Ascended Being — all in all one of the most challenging adversaries the world will ever face.

Above: A scientist's work is never done.

human-built fighter plane retro-engineered from Goa'uld technology. I still remember the look on Brad's face when I pitched the idea of having to strap an active Stargate to the 302, and fly it out into space to prevent it from exploding on Earth. He looked at me like I was insane for a painfully long time, and eventually said, 'OK.' At this point I thought *he* might have lost his mind!"

For Tony Amendola, the experience of meeting up with not so old friends was quite the thrill. "It was fun working with Neil Denis again," he says. "I was watching Rya'c literally grow up because every time I see him, he is three or four inches taller! The first time we met him, way back when, he was just a boy. Now he's rapidly becoming a man, and it's lovely to actually be part of that." The actor confirms that the companionship was warm, but the temperature was not. "There was a lot of night shooting in those episodes, and lots of big explosions. Sometimes you space out a little bit at night, because it gets so cold. But with that one — the explosions were so big, and the running was so energising, I mean, we were hightailing it out of there! We were really *moving*, so there was no question of getting cold." ⋏

REDEMPTION [PART II]

Written by: Robert C. Cooper Directed by: Martin Wood	Guest cast: Tony Amendola (Bra'tac), Christopher Kennedy (Dr Larry Murphy), David Hewlett (Dr McKay), Garry Chalk (Colonel Chekov), Neil Denis (Rya'c), Gary Jones (Sgt Davis), Tobias Mehler (Lt Simmons), David Palffy (Anubis)

E arth is under a sustained assault from Anubis, and faces imminent destruction as a power build-up in the Stargate threatens a chain reaction that will ultimately destroy the planet. As Sam Carter desperately seeks a scientific solution with the help (or hindrance) of her arch rival Rodney McKay, Teal'c, Bra'tac and Rya'c stage a daring physical assault on the energy weapon *in situ*. When Teal'c is captured by Anubis's forces, things look bleak for the Tauri, until help arrives from an unexpected source. Back on Earth, Jonas's lateral thinking results in Jack O'Neill and the X-302 being pressed into action once again, in a last ditch effort to save the planet — but at what cost to the Stargate programme?

Jonas

"I just want to be given the opportunity to prove that I can make a difference."

Amanda Tapping had one main reason to love this episode: "I got to do a lot of stuff with the scientist played by David Hewlett. Carter and McKay had this great antagonistic thing going on! David and I have a wonderful relationship, and I always enjoy playing with him, because he's an actor's actor in the sense that he'll throw something out — whether it's a look, or a snide remark — and I'll throw something back. It's like chucking a ball back and forth. He's a very, very funny man. He's also really smart, so it's fun to play that element."

Director Martin Wood also loved the episode: "It is one of my favourite shows because it has the X-302. Both Brad and I have a passion for fighter jets, and we had the thrill of our lives going up in two T38 Airforce jets. After we'd gone up, Brad said he was going to write a show that had T38s in it, and promised to bring the pilots up to Vancouver. So 'Redemption' was partly born from the fact that Brad wanted to say thanks. In the episode you see guys getting in and out of planes, and those are actually the pilots we flew with. Han Joachim Ruff was with Brad, and the blond one is Joe Simile, who was with me. We called these guys and said, 'Hey, bring the planes up.' They landed them in

Vancouver after a *tremendous* amount of red tape. You can imagine — landing American fighter jets in a Canadian airport! We put them in the background of all the shots.

Above: Once more unto the breach, dear friends...

"When I was originally told what was going to happen, I decided we were going to take the X-302 out and have our guys climb all over it," Wood continues. "Andy Mikita came up with a great idea. He suggested we put it on the back of a flatbed truck, and drive it out of the hanger so that in the shot it looks like it taxies itself out.

"Rick and Amanda *loved* being in the X-302," the director reveals. "There's all these controls, and they were driving around just pushing buttons and flicking switches. The other thing they liked was that when they put the masks on, it didn't matter what they said, as we would dub it in later. They didn't have to get the lines right. I mean, they did (sort of), but it was so funny. I loved everything about that episode — doing the flying sequences, and all the other cool stuff. It was just too brilliant." ⅄

DESCENT

Written by: Joseph Mallozzi and Paul Mullie
Directed by: Peter DeLuise

Guest cast: Carmen Argenziano (Jacob Carter/Selmak), Colin Cunningham (Major Davis), Gary Jones (Sgt Davis), John Shaw (Dr Friesen), Peter DeLuise (Lt Dagwood)

Jacob Carter and Major Davis accompany SG-1 on a salvage mission to investigate an apparently deserted Goa'uld mothership that has arrived in Earth orbit. The mystery deepens as the team discovers evidence of a violent assault on the computer core, which has been sealed off. The self-destruct sequence has been suspended, and the abandoned vessel appears to be Anubis's ship, from which they recently rescued the Asgard Supreme Commander, Thor. Before the team is able to regain control of the vessel, the drive controls are disabled and the mothership plunges into the North Pacific...

Hammond to Teal'c

"We've all been holding our breath down here."

"That is most unwise."

Brad Wright is proud of the fact that every season, *Stargate SG-1* tries to push the envelope and do something that's incredibly ambitious for television. Season six was no exception, with 'Descent' being just one of those minor miracle events. "This episode grew out of my desire to do some stuff underwater," he says. "For my underwater scenes, we sunk a mothership in the Pacific Ocean, that's all! You can get great underwater scenes in the movies, but to get that level of authenticity in a television show is a major triumph of achievement. I'm immensely proud of everyone concerned in the production."

The producer is particularly impressed with the way Corin Nemec managed to hold his breath for an inordinate amount of time to complete a memorable — and quite literally breathtaking — underwater sequence in one swim. "We weren't even sure that Corin *could* swim, until someone reminded us he had been a lifeguard," Wright recalls. "But when he did the underwater swim he held his breath for almost two minutes. We tried to do it in the office and couldn't manage it, and we were just sitting down resting. He had to do all the physical stuff, *and* hold his breath. Hats off to him for that."

Sadly, not all the cast were as competent in the water. Amanda Tapping laughs, "The scene called for us to be surrounded by rising water, and we had to find an air pocket. So, as the set sinks and the water rises, we're dropping our vests and stuff so that we can float to

Above: Carter and O'Neill get that sinking feeling.

the surface, and it's all going well. Then the ceiling hits, but we find this air pocket. The idea was for us to stick our heads up and breathe, but what I kept forgetting to do was tilt my head all the way back. So I'd feel the water just above my nose and I'd open my mouth to take a breath and I'd choke. It happened about three times in a row! So after three takes, Richard turns to me and says, 'Why do you keep doing that?' So I smacked him and said, 'It's not like I'm doing it on purpose!' all girly-like. I was so completely embarrassed. But it works in the scene, because when the water lowers and it looks like I'm choking, I was, in actual fact, choking..."

Known for his cameo roles, Peter DeLuise admits that he did not get his hair wet in this episode: "I was not in the water. I was one of the navy fellows who came in the pod and waited by the escape tubes for them to return. It's a little hard to read on my uniform, but my name in 'Descent' is Dagwood — which was my character from *SeaQuest*. It was a fun little inside thing. I still have that Dagwood patch!" ⅄

FROZEN

Written by: Robert C. Cooper	Guest cast: Venus Terzo (Dr Francine Michaels), Bruce
Directed by: Martin Wood	Harwood (Dr Osbourne), Paul Perri (Dr Woods), Dorian
	Harewood (Thoran), Ona Grauer (Ayiana), Gary Jones
	(Sgt Davis)

A chilly house call awaits Dr Fraiser as she joins SG-1 on a return trip to the site of the Antarctic Stargate. Scientists working at the site have unearthed a human female preserved deep in the ice, and the discovery threatens to undermine the basic theories of human evolution. During the thawing process, the body shows signs of life. The proposed autopsy is quickly abandoned in favour of emergency room procedures, as Fraiser battles to resuscitate her new patient. As a storm closes in, members of the team start to fall sick with a mysterious illness and the base is placed under quarantine until a cure can be found.

Michaels to Carter

"That's impossible!"

"We've seen stranger."

First make-up assistant Dorothee Deichmann seems such a nice woman but says, "'Frozen' stands out for me because I was able to do frostbitten hands and feet, which we made really gory with lots of blisters and yucky things! I actually did one foot, and one of my colleagues did the other. Paul Perri, who played Dr Woods, was my foot." As well as chilled pedicures, the talented lady also worked on the ice maiden herself: "We had a lot of fun because she was cast in this slab of ice. I made her look frozen and we put melted ice over her, so it looked as though she was slowly defrosting." In order to create such a subtle yet powerful effect Deichmann explains, "They showed us a piece of art the production design people had done [see page 133], which had her half in the ice, with half of her face defrosted — so we knew what they were looking for. I also had an idea of where I wanted to go with it, and Jan Newman our make-up supervisor put in her five cents' worth too, so it all turned out the way the producers wanted, and looked really nice. I think the lights took a little bit away from my colours, but that's just me being picky!"

Amanda Tapping's memories of the episode are somewhat peculiar. "To make the operation room look all insulated, they lined it with bubble wrap. I'm talking the *big* stuff," she beams. "Now I'm a bubble wrap fanatic, as is Christopher Judge, so the two of us are like, 'Yay!

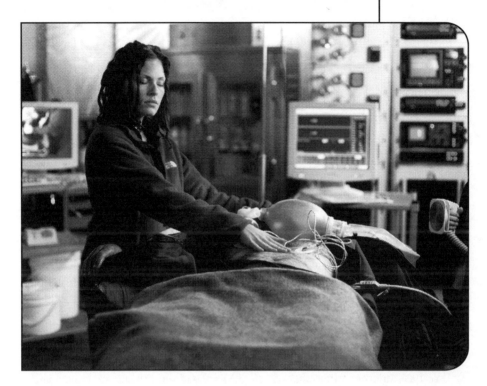

Above: An Ancient's power restored.

Bubble wrap!' and we were throwing ourselves against the wall laughing our heads off! Or we'd be sitting with a bit we'd pulled from the wall, happily going 'Phtt, phtt, phtt' and bursting this stuff. So now you know, next time you watch the episode, that in behind all that medical stuff is big, beautiful bubble wrap."

Guest actress Venus Terzo comments, "The thing I remember most is the jokester attitude of the cast. There was a lot of laughter involved. Christopher Judge was the worst! He kept standing behind me and making me laugh, and when I chided him he claimed that kind of behaviour was written into his contract. I almost believe him…"

The jacket Amanda Tapping wore in the show had a bit of a polar adventure once the show had wrapped. "One of our crew, Amy Gibbons, is an amazing adventurer and she flew up to the North Pole," Tapping says, "and actually found some uncharted islands! Anyway, when she went I asked if she could take my jacket, and have her picture taken at the North Pole." Tapping treasures the photo, which shows Amy duly wearing the jacket, holding up a sign that says 'Hello Amanda', with the degrees of latitude and longitude written alongside. ⋏

NIGHTWALKERS

Written by: Joseph Mallozzi and Paul Mullie	Guest cast: Blu Mankuma (Sheriff Knox), Vincent
Directed by: Peter DeLuise	Gale (Deputy/Agent Cross), Michael Eklund (Dark Haired Man), Peter Anderson (Dr Richard Flemming), Adrian Holmes (Special Ops Sgt)

Carter receives a mysterious phone call in the middle of the night from a respected geneticist, who claims that the project initiated by Adrian Conrad, the renegade Goa'uld, is running out of control. In the absence of O'Neill, Carter takes command of the team. Accompanied by Teal'c and Jonas, she travels to the sleepy fishing town of Steveston to investigate. Working with the local police, the team quickly establishes that the geneticist has died in suspicious circumstances. In the course of their enquiries, they discover an unidentified drug which could be the key to finding the killer. As SG-1 meet with increasing hostility from the locals, they become convinced that the town has a sinister secret to hide...

Stargate meets the *Men in Black*! "*Night of the Living Dead* was actually the inspiration for this one," counters director Peter DeLuise. "'Nightwalkers' also marks the first episode in which Richard Dean Anderson was not in a single frame, except for the opening credits." Explaining he goes on, "We had limited access to Rick. The fans thought that Richard wasn't going to appear in seven episodes. Yes, he had forty-two days off that year, which is what it takes to film seven episodes — but that didn't mean he wasn't going to appear in seven episodes. In fact, the way that they scheduled his time was so clever that the only episode he didn't appear in at all was this one.

"This was our little *X-Files* rip-off — I mean homage — where we go to this sleepy little town of fisherpeople, and we get the cold stares from the locals," DeLuise continues. "We find out that the foetal larval Goa'uld from 'Desperate Measures', which have been cloned and would normally be allowed to mature in a Jaffa pouch, have taken over human hosts. However, their ability to take over the human host is very limited in that they have to wait for the host to fall asleep. Then, and only then, can they take over the body. So we find that a large portion of the community goes to sleep, their bodies are activated by the baby

Goa'uld that are inside of them, and they gather to create a spaceship so they can get off the planet. They then return to bed at dawn, and the people awake to find that they are quite tired and the quality of their sleep has not been good. So it's a cool little mystery that we unravel."

Above: Here come the men in black – galaxy defenders.

Barbie Tapping (I'm teasing) grins, "This was great fun, because Christopher, Corin and I got to wear *really* cool clothes!" On a more serious note she offers, "It was nice to do an Earth-based story. I know that there's a real rift in the fanbase, you know, 'Earth-based versus space stories: which is better?' It's an oft-analyzed point amongst the people here at *Stargate* too. But every once in a while you have to address what's happening on Earth. Whether there's been infiltration by the Goa'uld that we don't know of, for instance. Anyway, Christopher and I had such a gas playing the elements of our relationship in this episode. It was like, 'Hey, here's the new guy dipping his onion rings into his french fries.' We got to play off all these beats that were really funny. But OK, mainly it was the clothes: Chris got to wear this long leather coat, and I got to wear these leather pants which were really hot!" Yep! Barbie and Ken rule. ⅄

ABYSS

Written by: Brad Wright
Directed by: Martin Wood

Guest cast: Michael Shanks (Daniel Jackson), Dorian Harewood (Thoran), Cliff Simon (Ba'al), Gary Jones (Sgt Davis), Ulla Friis (Shallan), Patrick Gallagher (Jaffa Commander)

The Tok'ra symbiote temporarily inhabiting O'Neill forces him into a mysterious rescue mission in the heart of a Goa'uld stronghold. Caught and tortured by the System Lord Ba'al, O'Neill desperately tries to resist interrogation. An unexpected visit from Daniel Jackson, now an Ascended Being, gives O'Neill hope, but his friend is unable to use his powers to free him. Refusing Daniel's offer of ascension, O'Neill is tested to his limits as Ba'al exploits the sarcophagus technology to increase his torment. Knowing that the knowledge he holds could cost an innocent life, O'Neill asks Daniel to end his suffering permanently. Meanwhile, back at Stargate Command, the Tok'ra are being evasive, and the rest of SG-1 wage a war of wills with their allies to rescue Jack in time...

> **O'Neill**
>
> "If I'm catching the next plane of existence outta here, you've gotta give me something."

This episode was particularly harrowing for the good Colonel O'Neill, which was actually rather fitting as Richard Dean Anderson wasn't at his sparkling best during filming. "I don't think I was in too laughy a mood, because I'd just had some knee surgery. We had this set on gimbals that would move up and down, and because of the surgery I couldn't do the tumbling that I wanted to down the walls. So I was a little limited, and I'm not fond of limited in any way." There was one bright light on his horizon, though: "Working with Michael, I love. In fact he came back a couple of times in season six, and we've

Ba'al

Also known as Beelzebub, or Baalzebub, this very unpleasant soul was reputed to be one of the fallen angels of Satan. In keeping with his status as System Lord, Baal's name means Master, Owner, Lord, or God and he was thought to be responsible for droughts, plagues and other agricultural calamities — as well as making Jack O'Neill's lives a misery

had some great one-on-one scenes. The powers that control these things seem to like to put us both in a bag and shake it up. I really enjoy that aspect of working with him. He and I have an innate understanding of rhythm in our scenes. It's easy working with Michael, because you can look over at him and see the light is *on* — so it's all good."

Above: Daniel and Jack contemplate their time on Big Brother.

Mr Anderson had to look particularly unfit in this episode, and make-up supervisor Jan Newman admits, "Richard's make-up was quite the challenge, because normally he looks so good we don't have to do much to him at all. For this one we had to keep making him paler, because each time he was revived he was becoming more and more exhausted. By the end of it he looked *really* done in, which was great because it meant I had done my job!"

The episode also saw the expansion of the domain of yet another System Lord. Writer Paul Mullie says, "'Summit' was almost the audition for some System Lords. Not for performance, but for how they came across on screen — and I thought Ba'al was great. A lot of the fans agreed, so we brought him back for 'Abyss'." ʎ

Written by: Joseph Mallozzi and Paul Mullie Directed by: Peter DeLuise	Guest cast: Dean Stockwell (Dr Kieran), Joel Swetow (First Minister Valis), Doug Abrahams (Commander Hale), Gillian Barber (Ambassador Dreylock), Gary Jones (Sgt Davis), Rob Daly (Resistance Leader)

A message arrives from Kelowna requesting the establishment of trade relations with Earth. Although reluctant, given the recent events involving Daniel Jackson, the SGC is forced to consider the proposition in light of the potential benefits of having a reliable source of Naquadria. The negotiations are tense. The Kelownans seek only military technology in order to defend themselves from hostile forces on their home planet; whilst the SGC is resistant to the idea of supplying any kind of technology which may be used offensively. The Kelownans warn that they will unleash a hugely destructive Naquadria bomb as a pre-emptive strike against their enemies, unless defensive technology is supplied from Earth. Acting on information supplied by Dr Kieran, Jonas's former mentor, SG-1 travel to Kelowna to establish contact with a rebel faction, to see if a peaceful solution can be found to the crisis.

Teal'c

"I, too, was considered a traitor. What I did, I did for my people. In time they came to understand this."

"This was our first return visit to Kelowna," says Peter DeLuise. "The inspiration for the episode sort of came from A *Beautiful Mind*, that wonderful movie in which Russell Crowe's character imagines that he has a few extra friends than actually exist in real life. That's exactly what we had here. We had Dean Stockwell playing Jonas's mentor, and he believes that there is this ultra-secret rebellion going on — but it's really just the long-term effects of Naquadria on his sanity. He's lost it! I thought it was a fun episode in that we don't usually deal with somebody else's psychosis. Dean Stockwell is such a professional, by the

Naquadria

A more powerful version of Naquadah, the fuel used to fire up the Stargate. Pockets of this element have been found on Jonas Quinn's home planet. Highly unstable, it can be used to create weapons of mass destruction, but repeated exposure to minimal amounts can be hazardous — to the mind as well as body.

way. It was a great pleasure to work with him.

"Anyway, this was a return to Kelowna, to deal with what's going on with them," DeLuise continues. "It's the second of four Kelowna episodes, actually. The first is 'Meridian', when Daniel got the dose of radiation, and this is the second, in which we see how the government is put together, meet some of the other players on their planet, and learn that Naquadria plays such an important role and is an alternative super energy source. Now the next one is going to be the two-parter at the beginning of season seven: 'Fallen' and 'Homecoming'."

Realising that he probably shouldn't give too much away, DeLuise nevertheless goes on, "In that story we find that Jonas has been taken into captivity by Anubis, who tortures him with the same memory-sapping device he used on Thor. Anubis is made aware of this new power source, so he goes to try to find it himself. And then toward the end of season seven, well, I've just been handed a possible plotline, written by Corin Nemec himself. It's about the ongoing ill effects of the Naquadria experiments on the core of the Kelownan planet. They have a catastrophe that is threatening their whole planet's existence in that story. So that's the whole Kelownan arc." ᛉ

Above: Jonas shows discretion is the better part of valour.

THE OTHER GUYS

Written by: Damian Kindler	Guest cast: Patrick McKenna (Dr Jay Felger), John
Directed by: Martin Wood	Billingsley (Dr Simon Coombs), Adam Harrington
	(Khonsu), Michael Adamthwaite (Her'ak), Gary Jones
	(Sgt Davis), Martin Sims (Dol'ok), Randy Schooley
	(Meyers), Michael Dangerfield (Big Jaffa)

During an off-world mission babysitting some scientists, SG-1 are captured by the Goa'uld and taken to their mothership. One of the scientists, Felger, is an avid fan of SG-1, and manages to persuade his colleague Coombs to help rescue them. Our unlikely heroes stumble about on the Goa'uld ship, eventually finding SG-1, only to be met with a less than enthusiastic reception. SG-1 have allowed themselves to be captured to make contact with a Tok'ra agent, Khonsu, posing as a Goa'uld System Lord. As SG-1 are transported back to the planet by their captors, the scientists are hidden by Jaffa working with the Tok'ra. Unknown to the team, Her'ak, first prime of Khonsu, is aware that his master is Tok'ra, and has only been waiting for SG-1 to arrive to spring his trap.

Dr Felger

"There is something awfully hinky about this."

"'The Other Guys' was our comedy relief episode for the season," says executive producer Michael Greenburg. "It introduced some really fun characters. It was a bit of a departure for us, but once a year we get to do our own special brand of humour, and that was it."

The episode was *especially* special for Pat and his partner Jean, competition winners who had flown in to meet the cast and crew of their favourite show, courtesy of MGM and the nice people at Channel 4 television in the UK. The trip coincided with one of your intrepid author's set visits, so I met up with the lucky pair on board British Airways flight 085. The two could barely contain their excitement. "The flight crew have been fabulous," grinned Pat. "They are fans of *Stargate* too, and presented us with a bottle of champagne to congratulate us on winning the contest!" Spare copies of the *Stargate Illustrated Companion* volumes 1 and 2 just happened to be in my bag, so the pair received signed copies of those as well. (OK, they probably preferred the champagne.)

Upon arrival at their destination, our travellers were met by none other than Teryl Rothery. Hugs were exchanged, photos taken and

promises made to 'catch up' on set after a good night's sleep. Pat later confessed, "I didn't sleep a wink. I was far too excited." It was pouring with rain and blowing a gale. The location was a distinctly unglamorous old quarry, but were we downhearted? We most certainly were not. Their first day on location could have been marred by the severely inclement weather but in true British fashion, our pair was oblivious to the elements. Meeting their favourite stars, chatting with the crew and witnessing the special effects team's magic at first hand added up to what both Pat and Jean hailed as, "The best day of our lives." Pat was so inspired by the visit that he decided on a permanent reminder of his time there: "I'd been thinking of getting a tattoo, and once I'd been treated with such respect and warmth on set, I knew exactly the kind of design I'd choose." He turned up next day with a pattern resembling the Stargate on one bicep, and one similar to the SG-1 patch on the other. Now *that's* devotion for you. As the *Stargate* team bade farewell, Pat announced, "No matter what happens with the show, I will always treasure the time I spent with these guys. I want to remember this feeling for the rest of my life!" ⅄

Above: Teal'c, Coombs and O'Neill, en route *to the tattoo parlour.*

ALLEGIANCE

Story by: Peter DeLuise
Directed by: Peter DeLuise

Guest cast: Carmen Argenziano (Jacob Carter/Selmak), Tony Amendola (Bra'tac), Obi Ndefo (Rak'nor), Peter Stebbings (Malek), Link Baker (Artok), Rob Lee (Major Pierce), Kimani Ray Smith (Ocker), Herbert Duncanson (SG Guard), Dan Payne (Ashrak)

The destruction of a Tok'ra base causes Jacob to lead a dramatic evacuation of the survivors to the SGC's top secret Alpha site. SG-1 are required to act as peacemakers, as the natural distrust between the resident rebel Jaffa warriors and the newly arrived Tok'ra refugees causes tension between the two races. Tempers are frayed enough when Carter uncovers an act of sabotage which could have destroyed the base, but when a member of the Tok'ra is murdered the uneasy alliance threatens to boil over into serious confrontation. SG-1 and Dr Fraiser must uncover the perpetrator before the situation gets out of hand, and the tension between the two factions leads to outright hostility. When the real culprit is identified, all three races must work together in order to ensure their continued survival against a common enemy.

Bra'tac

> "This single blade did what we could not. It has brought us together."

"'Allegiance' — that was a fun episode," states Peter DeLuise. "We got to see the Alpha site, and got to see good-guy rebel Jaffa and good-guy Tok'ra behaving in *not* very good-guy ways! It's not like the Tok'ra's behaviour was totally unrecognisable though. They've all lived to be several hundred years old, whereas the Jaffa... well, the oldest one is only about 137, so they're just teenagers to the Tok'ra! Why should they treat them like equals? The Tok'ra have never had much time for the rebel Jaffas. Eventually, thanks to the actions of Bra'tac — who's so heroic and so selfless in his pursuit of justice and doing the right thing — they realize that the Jaffa are a formidable force, and *should* be treated as equals. Bra'tac makes that big speech at the end, as only Tony Amendola can do. He uses the metaphor of the knife — that this knife has brought us together, and has killed us equally. Now it must keep us together, as we have to join up to kill our common enemy. That was a really fun moment for me, because Tony really kicks ass when it comes to that kind of stuff!"

Tony Amendola puts much of his ass-kicking ability down to the script: "'Allegiance' was another one where the story around me was very sweet. It's the one that deals with racism, and there's an invisible enemy. We end up in a camp; gradually people are killed and at first you think it's me. The fight scenes were incredible," Amendola laughs. "I mean, when you're fighting with an invisible foe, you know, it's extra challenging. Generally when you fight there is another person there, you know.

"Brad Wright originally told me 'we have this episode and it's going to happen on this date', but then they had to move it for some reason to a week earlier," Amendola continues. "This was very difficult, because I was doing a stage production of *Cyrano*, and that had always been a dream for me. Brad understood that, and we chatted and found a way to make it work. They kind of bent the schedule a little bit. I really appreciated that, and was very moved by it actually. They could have re-written it so another person could have taken the role. But I thought it was important that Bra'tac did the job, and Brad agreed. The fact that he would adjust the schedule like that is rare. It's not something that is done very often for a recurring character, so I'm forever grateful." λ

Above: Carter checks the web for spare parts.

Written by: Damian Kindler Directed by: Andy Mikita	Guest cast: Peter Stebbings (Malek), Malcolm Stewart (Dollen), Gwynyth Walsh (Kelmaa/Egeria), Allison Hossack (Dr Zenna Valk), Daryl Shuttleworth (Commander Tegar)

The arrival of SG-1 is eagerly awaited on the planet Pangar, where the locals appear to have conquered all forms of disease and live in perfect health. The Pangarans have developed a drug called Tretonin, which makes the immune system impervious to any ailment. They appear eager to trade this knowledge in exchange for Gate addresses for known Goa'uld home worlds. In spite of their reservations, Carter and O'Neill return to Earth with a sample of Tretonin for testing, leaving Jonas and Teal'c to attempt to unlock the secrets of the wonder drug.

Dollen and O'Neill

"The leader of this group will be a brilliant and savvy negotiator. Personally I cannot wait to meet a man of such genius..."

"Howdy folks."

Damian Kindler describes how he found the 'Cure': "In January 2002, I pitched four ideas to the producers at *Stargate SG-1*, one of which was 'The Other Guys'. Of those four ideas I pitched, the first idea they didn't quite cotton to, the second idea we discussed for forty-five minutes, the third one was 'The Other Guys' and the fourth idea they didn't really care about. Robert Cooper told me they liked the two middle pitches, and they would call to tell me which one they wanted to buy. So when they called, it was to say they wanted me to do 'The Other Guys'. I was thrilled because I liked that the most.

"But the second pitch, the one we mulled over in the room for forty-five minutes, ended up being 'Cure'," Kindler continues. "It's about a civilization seeking the powers of a Goa'uld symbiote, and using them in kind of an edgy and unorthodox way. Naturally SG-1 say, 'You can't do that! You don't want to be *farming* these things.' That idea was what

Symbiotes

The larval state of the Goa'uld race, a symbiote is capable of repairing and sustaining human life for an extended period of time. These highly prized creatures are sought after by other aliens, NID representatives and sick individuals throughout the known worlds.

intrigued everyone in the room, and it was also touching on something Brad and Rob had wanted to do anyway. Once I wrote 'The Other Guys', and had been hired onto the show's writing staff, 'Cure' was the next one on my plate."

"I think of 'Cure' as a *Stargate* fan's *Stargate*," the writer says. "It touches on so many different elements of the science, of the mythology. It's also a very simple, stand alone, 'we go through the Gate, we meet a new bunch of people' episode. But it also has the density of a black hole! I think anyone who doesn't know the show is going to be reeling when they watch this one, because there is so much to figure out. Who are the Goa'uld? What is a symbiote? Ohmigosh — who are the Tok'ra? So the plot is like a switchback s-curve all the way through. It was a real challenge to write. It was beautifully directed by Andy Mikita, who did a superb job. The effects look great too. I'm really proud of it. It was one of those episodes that really got stuck into all the history and mythology of *Stargate*, and I loved it." Many of the fans did too. Smiling, Kindler remarks, "I usually get my discussion group intel from Joe Mallozzi, and he has mentioned to me that the fans were quite taken with it." ʎ

Above: Awaiting the arrival of a particularly eloquent guest.

PROMETHEUS

Written by: Joseph Mallozzi and Paul Mullie	Guest cast: George Wynter (Al Martell), Ian Tracey (Smith), Kendall Cross (Julia Donovan), Colin Cunningham (Major Paul Davis), Enid-Raye Adams (Jones), John de Lancie (Colonel Frank Simmons), Michael Shanks (Voice of Thor)
Directed by: Peter Woeste	

When an investigative journalist threatens to go public with information about the top secret *Prometheus* project, a serious breach of security is feared. In an attempt to avoid the story being leaked, the Pentagon agrees to allow the journalist a world exclusive. She will be granted unrestricted access to the *Prometheus* facility, but only in exchange for complete control over the timing of the release of the story. Reluctantly, Carter and Jonas meet the journalist and her film crew at the site of the project, located in a remote part of the Nevada desert. As the true nature and scale of the operation is revealed, some familiar faces from the past arrive to gatecrash the party. What begins as a conventional tourist tour suddenly turns into a desperate fight for survival.

O'Neill to Thor

"I thought you were going for the new body?"

"I did!"

"It's... nice."

Production designer Bridget McGuire beams with pride when asked about the subject of the episode, the custom-built *Prometheus*: "This project has probably been one of our most challenging of the year, and it certainly needed all of our collaborative ingenuity. We were asked to design a spaceship, which was great because spaceships are a lot of fun to design and build! In this instance, they wanted one that looked less like a hi-tech alien vessel, and more like one that had been built for the USAF. We decided to incorporate many of the features we see in military vessels today, and adapt them for space travel. Basically what we have with the *Prometheus* is a destroyer in space, so we started by looking at lots of elements from current sea-going military craft. The ship has the capacity to be an aircraft carrier, for the X-302, so we adapted some of the elements of an aircraft control tower. We also wanted to have a proper bridge, so we have this wonderful area that has the captain's chair, with navigation behind, and systems and operations up front along with the gunners. There's also the requisite big window that looks out into space. In the story, the ship is a work in progress," the designer confirms, "so there are

still elements waiting to become fully functional. We do have a control room for engineering, complete with consoles, monitors and the like."

The interior of the *Prometheus* was designed to resemble the inside of a submarine. "We've incorporated low ceilings, confined spaces and everywhere you look there's exposed conduits and piping," McGuire says. "It's a huge vessel, but if you really were on board with a full complement of crew, then it would be pretty claustrophobic."

The set for the *Prometheus* was anything but claustrophobic for the many fans who clambered in and out of the captain's chair and walked in awe along her corridors during the Gatecon 2002 studio tour. Over 100 people duly parked their bottoms, pressed buttons and stepped on and off the bridge during one of the highlights of the convention attendees' weekend. Alexandra Gmeiner from Germany said, "Even though I am in a wheelchair and this ship definitely wasn't built to accommodate it, I'm loving having the chance to be where my heroes will be. I can't wait to see the episode, then I can shout, 'I've been where O'Neill has been.' It will be so thrilling for me!" ⋏

Above: What do you mean, one of our ships is missing?

Written by: Brad Wright and Robert C. Cooper Teleplay by: Brad Wright Directed by: Andy Mikita	Guest cast: Patrick Currie (Fifth), Ian Buchanan (First), Kristina Copeland (Second), Rebecca Robbins (Fourth), Gary Jones (Sgt Davis), Dan Shea (Sgt Siler), Shannon Powell (Sixth)

The Asgard plan to trap every Replicator in the galaxy, with the use of a time dilation device, has failed. The Replicators have now overrun the Asgard home world. By creating a bubble in space where time moves more slowly, the Asgard had hoped to buy enough time to solve the long-standing problem of the Replicators once and for all — but something has gone seriously wrong. Not only is the time dilation device not working, its effects have been reversed, giving the Replicators a strategic advantage. At the request of Thor, SG-1 take the X-303 on its first mission. They venture into Replicator-dominated space, in order to repair and reactivate the dilation device before time quite literally runs out for the rest of the galaxy.

Carter to O'Neill

"We can't call it the *Enterprise*."

"Why not?"

Brad Wright starts out, "I wanted to introduce a new and powerful villain, that could one day take over from the Goa'uld as our main adversary. But I didn't want to have to come up with new aliens totally out of the blue. The human form of the Replicators are a wonderful extension of our mythos, but at the same time they are brand new — so it's the best of both worlds."

Director Andy Mikita says, "Two of the actors really stood out for me in this episode. Patrick Currie, who played Fifth, and Ian Buchanan, who played First. They were both great. Ian had a very, very powerful presence. He was absolutely terrifying, and so cold — almost Nazi-like. He played the whole thing not quite in a monotone, but in such a way that you could tell he was manufactured. In real life as it were, Ian was a treat to have

Replicators

The ultimate pest gone wild. Created as a defence mechanism, the little monsters are able to destroy entire worlds and civilizations. Originally spider-like superbugs, they have now evolved sufficiently to be able to take human form.

Above: SG-1 *receive some bad news from a good friend.*

around, and told us great stories about some of the big films he's been in, like *Panic Room*. Patrick Currie meanwhile is coming back for an episode of season seven called 'Space Race', in full prosthetic make-up this time."

The director also maintains that 'Unnatural Selection' "had some fantastic visual effects. We had a sequence on the planet's surface which was all shot green screen. We had the whole stage, basically three full walls of green screen, and the floor just had a sand treatment. We had some lightning effects and a bit of wind blowing to get the sense of feeling that we were outside, but that was it. It was a challenge for the actors because everything had to be in their imagination. We could describe how things were going to look, but we didn't have any proper design renderings to show. I take my hat off to everyone who did such a great job of making the episode look good."

Mikita also acknowledges the storyline itself: "It was a very nice turn of events to have a sympathetic alien. The ending to this episode was very haunting and was devised to leave us thinking, 'Aw! The poor guy!' but, of course, the Replicators are not humans, so they can't feel that way... or can they? There's always got to be a moral dilemma in any good story, and I'm very proud of the way we presented this one. This episode was definitely a personal favourite of mine." ⴷ

SIGHT UNSEEN

Written by: Ron Wilkerson
Teleplay by: Damian Kindler
Directed by: Peter Woeste

Guest cast: Jody Racicot (Vernon), Betty Linde (Mrs Sharpe), Gary Jones (Sgt Davis), Michael Karl Richards (Guardsman), Raimund Stamm (Hitchhike Driver), Jennifer Steele (Flight Attendant)

Jonas's sanity is called into question when he starts to see hideous creatures swarming over the SGC. As other base personnel begin to suffer from the same weird hallucinations, the investigation becomes focussed on an unidentified alien artifact retrieved by SG-1, which appears to be linked to the appearance of the creatures. Chaos descends as sporadic sightings outside Cheyenne Mountain cause widespread concern. As O'Neill forgoes a fishing trip in order to lead the containment team, the rest of the SGC work to find the source of the creatures, before mass hysteria leads to the existence of the Stargate being made public.

Jonas

"The possibility of being insane is interfering with my ability to relax."

Damian Kindler suggests that 'Sight Unseen' was almost bequeathed to him. "The guy who used to have my office, Ron Wilkerson, moved on to other things after season five," he says. "Before he left, he had pitched a concept of these things that people can't quite see in the SGC. Brad and Rob had worked on the story with him, and though they liked the plot, they knew Ron was busy and couldn't quite get a script to them on time because of scheduling issues. So they asked me to take the story they had developed with Ron, and do a teleplay.

"'Sight Unseen' ended up as quite an odd episode," Kindler muses. "It didn't quite materialise the way we all thought it would. It was sort of a screwy one, that some people might not like as much as other episodes, but I enjoyed writing it and I thought it had some great moments." Asked if he gets any say in who is cast in the roles he writes, Kindler offers, "I don't have a final say, but often they will ask for my input. They'll say, 'Hey, this is who we're thinking of — have you worked with them before?' Often I'll recognise actors from other shows that I've worked on and I'll say, 'Yeah! He's terrific!' or maybe 'This guy would be better.' I just throw my idea on the pile of other ideas. Ultimately Robert, Brad, Richard Dean Anderson and Michael Greenburg will make the final casting decision."

"I really like how Jody Racicot played Vernon. I had worked with Jody on an episode of *Kung Fu: The Legend Continues* quite some time ago, in Toronto. He was great then, plus I was quite taken with his audition for *Stargate* — I get to see the videotapes of the auditions. I thought Jody brought something very interesting to his role in 'Sight Unseen'."

Above: *O'Neill shows he'd rather be fishing.*

Aside from creating the cool creatures, visual effects supervisor Michele Comens has some very distinct memories: "We were filming the scene in the car. Michael Greenburg directed that little sequence. We had the stunt driver in the driver's seat, with the camera mounted right in front of him. Michael was in the passenger seat, the camera operator (who just sat there because the camera was mounted) was in the back seat, and myself and the camera assistant were squashed in the other back seat, with Ryan our second AD in the trunk almost. We were just holding on for dear life as Michael told the stunt driver to drive fast, brake fast and all this crazy stuff. By the end of two takes, I finally got out of the car. There is only so much a woman will do for her art!" ʎ

SMOKE AND MIRRORS

Written by: Kathryn Powers
Teleplay by: Joseph Mallozzi
and Paul Mullie
Directed by: Peter DeLuise

Guest cast: Ronny Cox (Senator Kinsey), Peter Flemming (NID Agent Malcolm Barrett), Jon Cuthbert (Agent Devlin), Colin Cunningham (Major Davis), Peter Kelamis (Dr Langham), John Mann (Luthor), Mi-Jung Less (Reporter)

enator Kinsey has been assassinated, and Jack is the assassin! Or that's how it appears, but of course we know there must be more going on. Sure enough, it turns out that the NID are up to their old tricks. A shadow group of businessmen, working within the NID, are using stolen alien devices which allow them to 'mimic' certain members of the SGC. With Jack in jail, the rest of SG-1 must prove his innocence, which leads Sam into an uneasy alliance with Barrett, an NID agent. Tracing the gun used in the assassination back to an arms dealer, they are able to identify the real shooter, but finding him turns out to be an explosive situation for Carter and Barrett. Sam finds out from her NID partner that Kinsey is alive, but also that an assassin wearing Major Davis's face is heading to the hospital...

> **O'Neill**
>
> "I wasn't on a mission. I was in Minnesota."

"'Smoke and Mirrors' is an NID plot to frame O'Neill for the assassination of Senator Kinsey," begins Peter DeLuise. "Joe and Paul wrote a great teleplay, based on the idea of the device which was used by the aliens in the episode entitled 'Foothold', way back in season three. If you recall, they were able to use the electronic devices to assume the identity of people." Showing himself to be every bit the fanboy, DeLuise smiles, "What I liked about the story is that the good guys scored a real victory. By uncovering what is happening with the whole NID subversive plot, the big players of the shadow government are arrested. From that we can assume that a large portion of the NID — maybe not all of them, but a large portion of them, the *rogue* part of the NID if you will — has been thwarted, or been arrested. I like to see a big resolution like that sometimes."

Fanboy hat still firmly on his head, DeLuise enthuses, "We also got to revisit the Barrett character, who we'd first met in 'Wormhole X-Treme!', and he's great. Peter Flemming plays Agent Barrett, and we like him a lot. He's a strong character." Returning to the plot for a moment, DeLuise frowns as he remembers, "Of course, unwittingly, by exposing all the goings on... because Senator Kinsey has been

shot, he's made out to be a martyr-type politician. This means his public rating goes way up, and we start to see some of the events that lead up to his election to high office. Not just to Senator but possibly the Vice-Presidency or even the Presidency. Mean old Kinsey is climbing the ladder there! And who better to play the part than Ronny Cox? He's just a joy."

Amanda Tapping thought working with Peter Flemming again was a cause for celebration too: "There's an interesting dynamic with Peter and I. It's not a love interest, because I hate the fact that every time a guy comes on the show Carter's supposed to fall in love with him — which means, of course, that he'll eventually die. Sam being the black widow of the *Stargate* universe! But there's an interesting relationship there, with us developing the trust issue. Does she trust him, or does she not? It's all good to work with." ⋏

Above: Danger – oily politician at work.

PARADISE LOST

Written by: Robert C. Cooper Directed by: Bill Gereghty	Guest cast: Tom McBeath (Colonel Harry Maybourne), Bill Dow (Dr Lee)

T he ubiquitous Maybourne returns, paying a surprise visit to Jack with an interesting proposition. He has information about a super weapon on a distant planet, knowledge that the NID have kept hidden from the SGC. Maybourne will give Jack the address, but only in return for a full pardon from the President. When it becomes apparent that they need the agent's co-operation, SG-1 is forced to bring Maybourne on the mission. As their 'assistant' tries to open the portal they think is guarding the weapon, he manages to overpower Carter. Maybourne escapes through the doorway, dragging O'Neill with him. Whilst Carter desperately tries to find a way to retrieve her colleagues, Maybourne and O'Neill arrive in an alien environment Maybourne believes is Utopia. Finding only remains, O'Neill begins to investigate what caused the inhabitants to apparently kill each other. Meanwhile, Maybourne becomes increasingly paranoid, forcing a deadly game of cat and mouse between our latter-day Robinson Crusoes.

O'Neill to Maybourne

"You ate my dog."

"In 'Paradise Lost', what happens is entirely my fault!" Amanda Tapping insists. "I had a hard time with that when I first read the script, but then I realised that things needed to be the way they were to facilitate the story — the majority of 'Paradise Lost' is simply O'Neill and Maybourne."

Tom McBeath thoroughly enjoyed his time working with Richard Dean Anderson once again. "I have to tell you about a particular incident that really made me laugh," he grins. "Jack is standing trying to fish, and I come up and throw an explosive into the water and the fish float to the surface, dead. Well, the day of the shoot, the explosive gets thrown into the water and the director says he wants us to keep going till he yells cut. So after the explosion, I wade into the water and eventually I reach out, grab one of the fish and throw it back to Jack. Then I go over to the other fish and throw them *all* back to Jack before wading back. I don't know how much of that they left in the final cut, but we just killed ourselves laughing afterwards because it was so silly! It was just a spur-of-the-moment action, born out of the need to do something with those fish that were floating there. It was especially hilarious as they used very stinky old fish!"

Whilst O'Neill and Maybourne were sharing some quality time,

Above: Cast away with only Maybourne for company.

Carter and Teal'c were doing the same. "This is the episode where Teal'c and Carter have a real moment," Amanda Tapping confirms. "She breaks down and cries and he comforts her, and it is just so warm and friendly. I think it's part of the nature of the development of these characters that we should finally be able to show our affection for each other. That yes, we're warriors, we're a team, and yes, we've come a long way in terms of 'you watch my back and I'll watch yours', but there's also a great love there. I mentioned it once in an interview about Carter's love for Teal'c, and it was misinterpreted as 'Ooo! Does that mean there's a sexual interest?' No! It means that these are two people who rely on each other heavily. He's my family. I'd kill for him and he'd kill for me, and if I'm upset he is going to comfort me. So we got to play that wonderful moment. Christopher and I really looked forward to doing it, and I think it played well."

Michael Greenburg cites 'Paradise Lost' as his "second favourite of the season", and has special praise for the music: "Joel Goldsmith did a phenomenal job scoring that show. It was a really great episode to start with, but he made it even better with his score." λ

METAMORPHOSIS

Written by: James Tichenor and Jacqueline Samuda Teleplay by: James Tichenor Directed by: Peter DeLuise	Guest cast: Jacqueline Samuda (Nirrti), Alex Zahara (Eggar), Dion Johnstone (Wodan), Raoul Ganeev (Lt Col Sergei Evanov), Gary Jones (Sgt Davis), Alex Rae (Alebran), Jaquie Janzen (Lt Rush), Dan Payne (Jaffa Commander)

When the Russian team brings an unauthorised visitor back through the Stargate, the SGC finds out that the Goa'uld Nirrti has been up to her old tricks. Experimenting on the inhabitants of the planet Alebran, she has created a machine that changes DNA, with disastrous results for her test subjects. Going to the planet, SG-1 discover the terrible mutated legacy of Nirrti's research, as she tries to create the perfect human host. Intending to free her victims, SG-1 discovers the people of the planet believe the System Lord to be a god, and their one chance of salvation. Using their extraordinary powers, Nirrti's followers imprison SG-1. The team finds itself subjected to genetic tampering, and Jonas gets some surprising insight into his own heritage. As Carter's life hangs in the balance, it's up to O'Neill to convince the people of Alebran of Nirrti's treachery, before it's too late.

Wodan to Teal'c

"Nirrti is curing us of our sickness."

"That is most unlikely."

Visual effects supervisor James Tichenor returns to his former life as a writer with this episode. "In the past, I had been a writer, before I started concentrating on visual effects," he reveals. "In fact, I'd worked with Brad when he was a freelance writer as well — that's how we knew each other — so it was kinda cool that he was willing to give me the chance to do some more writing. I pitched him an idea which was very different from what 'Metamorphosis' ended up being. Essentially, in the episode, we go to a planet that we're told is controlled by Nirrti, and she is doing genetic experiments on the people there. My original idea had people with wings, and people with serious super-powers who could jump fifty feet in the air — but the flip side was that they were falling apart genetically, and were very unstable. Of course, SG-1 would go in to help them. In the meantime, Jacqueline Samuda had pitched an idea to Brad, which had elements that would complement my story. Then basically what happened was that we spent a lot of time on the outline. We did one draft, and then Brad took it and re-wrote it."

What eventually came out contained a bunch of new characters and became a rather different plot, but essentially the original pitch was there. Between us we turned out a pretty cool story."

Above: Nirrti's unfortunate victims.

Peter DeLuise has a few words to say about the not so nasty side of Nirrti: "Jacqueline Samuda came up with some good ideas for the show. She is a pleasure to work with, plus she can wear those very tight dresses. She can just wear the crap out of them! And she has the best dirty look I've ever seen. Her face is wonderful. She's very graceful and very still — it's all about the power of the eyes. She could scare you to death! I *loved* the stare-off between her and Fraiser over Cassandra, back in 'Rite of Passage'."

To the director's chagrin, the character bites the dust toward the end of the episode. "Unfortunately we see her get her neck broken and thrown to the ground," he concedes. "But hey, her larvae could have crawled out and found another body. But then it wouldn't be Jacqueline... Mind you, Goa'ulds have sustained people with broken necks before, so maybe she got up after that, and will come back sometime. I'm in denial that she's dead." ⅄

DISCLOSURE

Written by: Joe Mallozzi and Paul Mullie **Directed by:** Bill Gereghty	**Guest cast:** Ronny Cox (Senator Kinsey), Colin Cunningham (Major Davis), Garry Chalk (Colonel Chekov), Martin Evans (British Ambassador), Francois Chau (Chinese Ambassador), Paul Batton (French Ambassador), Dan Payne (Jaffa Commander)

The international community is becoming increasingly suspicious of the number of galactic 'incidents' being explained away by the American and Russian governments. In an attempt to preserve the support of key nations, representatives from China, France and Great Britain are invited to the Pentagon for a top secret briefing on the Stargate programme. Senator Kinsey tries to take advantage of the situation by attempting to undermine the leadership of General Hammond, and the work undertaken at the SGC. His clear intention is to try to wrest control of the Stargate programme from the military, placing it under the auspices of the civilian-run NID. General Hammond has a fight on his hands to justify the actions of his flagship team to a sceptical audience.

Thor to Kinsey

"O'Neill suggested I send you to a distant planet... but I am reasonably certain his statement was in jest."

Acknowledging that clip shows aren't universally recognised as the best examples that episodic television has to offer, Joe Mallozzi nevertheless has nothing but praise for this episode's director: "Bill Gereghty directed it, and did a wonderful job. I mean, let's face it, clip shows don't tend to be very visual episodes, but Bill did phenomenal work putting this one together."

Paul Mullie explains, "In this particular episode we tried as best we could to focus on some of the grander visual effects that we've done, to make it a kind of a 'best of' visual effects. So we had ships crashing, we had stuff blowing up... We also tried to get in as many clips from episodes Joe and I wrote as possible." The reason for this, the cheeky writer reveals, "is that you actually get paid by how many of the pages have come from your other episodes, so we really did our best to get as many of ours in as we could. But then Brad Wright got ahold of it and added a whole bunch of other clips from other people's episodes, which was totally unnecessary as far as I was concerned." Mullie also says, "Some people may say that whenever you

opt to do a clip show you're telling the audience what they already know, while others say it's a way of revisiting favourite moments. I don't know which is right. What I do say is that it's all in the eye of the beholder."

Joe Mallozzi counters with, "You can say what you like about clip shows, but when you have to write one and you don't have any choice, you try to do your best to make the 'frame' plot — the device upon which the clips hang — a good, solid story. So we came up with Senator Kinsey trying to take political control of the SGC using these foreign ambassadors as a way to wrest control from the Air Force, and put it into the hands of an organisation that he ultimately would be overseeing. Having Ronny Cox's character sparring with Don Davis's character made the episode a cut above a simple clip show, because not only was there a story, there was real drama! It was fascinating watching them trying to outplay each other."

Mullie concludes, "It was actually Brad and Robert who came up with the idea of Thor showing up at the end. That added another special element, and was a fun little moment." λ

Above: Defending the Stargate programme?

FORSAKEN

Written by: Damian Kindler	Guest cast: Martin Cummings (Aden Corso), David
Directed by: Andy Mikita	Paetkau (Liam Pender), Sarah Deakins (Tanis Reynard), Dion Johnstone (Warwick Trevor), Trevor 'Grizz' Jones (Second Alien), Bruce Dawson (Serberus Crewman)

Whilst on a scientific survey, O'Neill and the rest of SG-1 stumble across a crashed spacecraft called the *Serberus*. They soon meet the surviving members of her crew, who claim to have been marooned on the planet for some time. The team offers to help repair the ship, in the hope of developing positive diplomatic relations with yet another friendly race. When the wreck comes under attack, the team fights alongside their new allies to protect the vessel, but the extreme violence demonstrated by their new companions makes SG-1 uneasy. As Carter and Jonas flirt their way to the truth, Teal'c and O'Neill investigate the crash site. What they discover on the planet leads them to reconsider the wisdom of their offer of assistance...

Aden to Carter

"You're an officer, a scientist, an explorer and, apparently, a pretty fair mechanic."

"And I make a mean soufflé..."

Christopher Judge considers 'Forsaken' to be one of the season's most memorable episodes. "The team kind of get fooled by appearances," he begins. "We eventually come across the real protagonists, but because their appearance is different we don't take them at face value. God love us, *Stargate* is not a 'message show' by any stretch of the imagination, but occasionally there are messages in there. Our writers are so good about not beating people over the head with them, and this really was one of those times where that restraint worked very well."

If proof were needed that *Stargate* writers often work above and beyond the call of duty for their craft, 'Forsaken' is a prime example. "This was a bit of a challenge," laughs Damian Kindler, "because I literally wrote the script while I was on vacation up in Ontario, in a cottage on an island. I remember I was sitting in this boathouse looking out at the blue, glistening water, cocooned in solitude with my laptop. 'Forsaken' was one of those scripts that Rob Cooper and I thought added a cool alien twist to a really great story. When I think about the episode, I remember the *astounding* performance from Dion Johnstone. Then, of course, there was

Above: Comrades in arms.

the amazing ship design by the art department." Balancing his enjoyment of the finished product with the effort it took to get there, Kindler remembers that "it was an episode that I really put *so* much work into. I was under a lot of pressure time-wise. I'm sure you know what it's like when you've come back from vacation — you've been away for two weeks, and everyone has moved on to something else. So it was really just me on this script. We perhaps didn't get the same quality that's apparent when everybody is together, and you're bouncing ideas off each other." That said, Kindler is adamant that the experience was all good: "I don't want you to think that I have any ill feeling towards 'Forsaken'. On the contrary, I think of it as a real adventure." Revealing just a tiny little spoiler he nods, "We may be bringing back the character of Warwick in season seven. Any time someone comes in and says, 'Hey, we want to use elements from an episode you've written', then you know you haven't done too bad a job. So I'm proud of 'Forsaken'. I think Andy Mikita directed it brilliantly. It stands up as a pretty strong episode, though being picky, I think it could have used a few more brains on it." ᛉ

THE CHANGELING

Story by: Christopher Judge
Teleplay by: Brad Wright
Directed by: Martin Wood

Guest cast: Michael Shanks (Daniel Jackson), Musetta Vander (Shaun'ac), Tony Amendola (Bra'tac), Peter Williams (Apophis), Carmen Argenziano (Jacob Carter/Selmak), John Ulmer (Firefighter), Gianna Patton (Nurse)

T eal'c's sense of reality is thrown into confusion when he finds himself slipping in and out of what appears to be another life. Not only is he human and married to a former lover in this alternate existence, he's also part of a group of firefighters who bear an uncanny resemblance to his fellow SG-1 team-mates. As he continues to slip between these two apparent realities, Teal'c naturally begins to fear for his sanity. Help comes from an unexpected source: will Daniel be able to persuade his friend that there is another explanation for what he has been experiencing? As Teal'c struggles to understand what is happening to him, on a planet far, far away another battle is being waged. One that threatens not only Teal'c's life, but that of his old mentor, Bra'tac.

> **Teal'c**
>
> "I would prefer not to consume bovine lactose at any temperature."

Ask anyone at *Stargate* to identify one specific memorable episode, and the likelihood is they'll answer 'The Changeling'. Charmingly modest about his role in bringing the story to the screen, Christopher Judge delares, "Anytime you write something, you're always worried about how it's going to be perceived. But everyone gave this 150 per cent. It was just so nice to get the feeling that everybody enjoyed it. After all, it was a very different episode of *Stargate*."

Totally delighted with the finished product, Judge comments, "First of all — let's face it — my track record of being dependable and responsible and all that hasn't been the greatest. For Brad to go out on a limb and take an entire episode, and basically let me do it totally without conforming to the checks and balances that go along with the script-writing process — well, I think Brad's crazy and a lunatic! Seriously though, for him to have that trust in me is incredibly heartwarming. Then for Brad to polish it and make it so much better was wonderful." The actor grins, "Everyone in every department just outdid themselves, bringing their own ideas and their own specialities and subtleties. It was really nice because on a daily basis, people

Above: Teal'c wakes up and smells the coffee — or does he?

would come up and say 'maybe we can do this?' or 'maybe we could try that'. It was a fantastic experience.

"We were shooting it round about my birthday and Alan, my husband, got to play a fireman!" Amanda Tapping reveals. "Well, Christopher's girl-friend Gia was going to be a nurse in the show, so I said Alan would make a great fireman. Suddenly the producers got involved, and Alan was like, 'Well, OK… what do I have to do?' He's not in the business, so he didn't want to do anything that made him look silly. But he did it, and he looked as cute and sexy as hell! He got to spend two days doing what I do, so he now has a much clearer picture of my job. By the third day, when I had to get up at 5am but he didn't, he said to me, 'I don't know how you do it!'"

"We were shooting the scene where we were by the water, and Chris and I were near death," recalls Tony Amendola. "We were lying there, and all of a sudden a breaker would come in and we would all have to get up and run to avoid getting soaked. The salmon were leap-ing up out of the river and I said to Chris, 'You know, I always knew this was a popular show, but now I know it's *really* popular. Even the salmon are jumping up to get a peek!'" ʎ

MEMENTO

Written by: Damian Kindler	Guest cast: John Novak (Col William Renson), Robert
Directed by: Peter DeLuise	Foxworth (Ashwan), Miguel Fernandes (Kalfas), Ingrid
	Kavelaars (Major Erin Gant), Alex Diakun (Tarek
	Solamon), Ray Gallett (Navigator)

All is going according to plan on the *Prometheus*'s shakedown cruise, until a technical hitch almost cripples the ship. SG-1 manage to get her working well enough to limp to an alien world with a Stargate that is the only chance they have of returning home. Unfortunately, 'Deny Everything' seems to be the local population's preferred point of view — until one intrepid soul decides to help.

Peter DeLuise reveals that the joy of directing this episode lay not just with the fact that he got to play with a big spaceship, but with the gentle but firm message the story offered. "Traditionally, when we go to a planet, we talk to the people who are in an arrested state of development," he points out. "They say, 'We have a god and we're waiting for him to come back,' and what we usually do is say, 'Well, your god is false and you need to move on.' Then we try to dissuade them from their history. The difference here is that the poeple deny their own history. So what we learn from this is to 'acknowledge your history, but don't be censored by it, or stopped by it'. It was a really neat lesson that Damian came up with."

Back in fanboy mode, DeLuise grins, "'Memento' was an episode where we take the *Prometheus* out for a test run, with a full compliment of crew. Now we had seen *Prometheus* previously, but this was the ship in full working order and ready to go! It was a lot of fun being able to do our own *Star Trek*-type thing. We've purposely avoided doing a big spaceship show before now — we had a Stargate! — so to end up doing one was a bit ironic. But Damian Kindler came up with this great idea… I blame him."

Mr Kindler is delighted to be held responsible and admits, "It was a real ship episode. Not 'shipp as in relationship (as fans talk about online), but ship as in *Prometheus*! I think it's a really cool episode in the sense that it incorporates where we started the show, with the raising of the Gate in Giza. We reflect on that imagery, and then we see how far

we've come in six years — we've built our own spaceship with hyper-drive engines with the USAF logo on the side."

Entering into the *Stargate* mutual admiration society, Kindler maintains, "I so love the direction Peter chose to take on the show. He found some incredible images: you could just take stills from the episode and put them on your walls as photographs! I'm thinking of the Gate with the sand dripping off it — just gorgeous stuff. Then he had all those amazing shots in space, with the ship dropping out of hyperspace. Fantastic."

Apparently there are some slightly less awe-inspiring images to be found if you watch the episode closely enough. Says Kindler, "There are also more metal briefcases in the background than you'll ever see in your life. If you watch and listen to the audio commentary when season six comes out on DVD you'll get what I mean. Peter and I did the commentary, and at one point I make a comment about this wealth of metal briefcases. I start counting these things and I'm like, 'How many *are* there?' Peter just says, 'Yes… we needed a lot of them.' Go figure!" ⅄

Above: Teal'c and Jonas enjoy a rare moment of calm.

PROPHECY

Written by: Joseph Mallozzi and Paul Mullie Directed by: William Waring	Guest cast: Thomas Kopache (Ellori), Victor Talmadge (Mot), Tom Schotte (Chazen), Rob Lee (Major Pierce), Sarah Edmondson (Natania), Johannah Newmarch (Sina), Karin Konoval (Dr Van Deusen), Brendan McClarty (Sendear)

When trying to liberate P4S 237 from the tyranny of Ba'al, SG-1 uncover a plot to overthrow the System Lord from within his own ranks. Before they can act on this new information, the team is forced to return to the SGC, as Jonas falls unconscious after experiencing a vision. Initially sceptical of his claim to be able to see into the future, they are soon persuaded of his precognitive abilities. Carter and Jonas speculate that these new powers may be the result of Nirrti's most recent DNA experimentation to create an advanced human host. Discovering a brain tumour, Dr Fraiser recommends immediate surgery to remove the growth before the intra-cranial pressure kills Jonas. But the patient is reluctant to give up what might be a valuable advantage to the SGC in the ongoing battle against the Goa'uld.

> **Fraiser to Jonas**
>
> "You might want to consider the possibility that you are valuable enough already."

Show co-producer and writer Joe Mallozzi begins, "Looking back, I think this was the best episode that Paul and I wrote for the sixth season. It was a tricky script to write. In fact, we wanted to create a situation where, in the end, we didn't necessarily have to answer the question we had set up at the beginning."

'Prophecy' is certainly an episode that has led to a lot of questions, mainly from fans who aren't quite sure what they have, or haven't, just watched. But if you think you're confused, rest assured that the writers had to go through a fair bit of head scratching as well. "I remember going over the script where Jonas has these 'flash forwards'," Mallozzi continues, "and we were struggling to come up with that pivotal moment where you know something major is off. We were trying to think of what makes the difference between when you see something happen, and when you question something you see happen. We were talking about maybe seeing Carter kill O'Neill, or looking at the possibility of O'Neill being revealed as an alien — all sorts of ridiculous scenarios! In the end though, Paul came up with the idea of the horn at the end, which played in the final version."

Mallozzi continues, "We were watching the cuts and the dailies and thought that this device wasn't obvious enough, and that people wouldn't pick up on it. But I've read online since that a lot of fans loved it, and caught on to it right away. It was that little twist that really made the show." Paul Mullie also offers that the episode "was an opportunity for Corin Nemec to show off his acting abilities. It was nice to see just what he could come up with."

In conclusion Mallozzi reiterates, "'Prophecy' was a hard script to write, and to finally come up with a twist that worked was a source of great relief and a certain amount of pride. It was one of those episodes where we wanted to have our cake and eat it. We wanted to ask, 'Was it a self-fulfilling prophecy? Did he make it happen by seeing it in the future?' — that kind of thing. From the debate I've seen online, I think we succeeded!"

Above: *Chazen eagerly awaits Lord Mot.*

FULL CIRCLE

Written by: Robert C. Cooper
Directed by: Martin Wood

Guest cast: Michael Shanks (Daniel Jackson), Alexis Cruz (Skaara), David Palffy (Anubis), Sean Amsing (Tobay), Vince Crestejo (Yu the Great), Michael Adamthwaite (Herak), Veena Sood (Abydonian Leader)

O ur favourite archaeologist returns to support the people of Abydos, and warn his old team-mates that Anubis, who is looking for The Eye Of Ra, one of the six 'Eyes of the Gods', is coming to Abydos in search of it. To stop Anubis unleashing the combined force of these ancient relics, the team must find the missing artifact before he can get his hands on it. Teal'c and the Abydonians battle against almost insurmountable odds to hold Anubis's army at bay. Meanwhile Daniel treads a fine line, as he tries to help his friends find The Eye without breaking the rules of non-interference by which his ascended self is bound...

Daniel

"You won't be alone."

A highly emotional time for all involved in the production of the show over the years, 'Full Circle' looked, at the time it was made, as though it was going to be the last ever episode of the show. A big fan of *Stargate SG-1* since day one (I first visited the set during the filming of the pilot), I'd like to share my own 'Full Circle' experience.

Mad Martin Wood (so called because of his penchant for epic episodes and pleasantly eccentric behaviour) had threatened to put me on screen as a scantily clad Goa'uld handmaiden during my visit to the set of 'The Other Guys'. Fortunately, I escaped that delight by drawing attention to my less than handmaidenly shape. "I'll do it next time," I promised, "but only if you put me in a tent!" — by which I meant a nice, big, all-encompassing garment, as befits my rather more matronly demeanour. "Sure!" yelled the Martian. I went home, and promptly forgot about the whole thing. Next time I arrived in Vancouver, Martin announced that arrangements had been made for my son Stuart and me to be in our favourite show, and that we should proceed to hair and make-up! "I told you I'd only do it if you put me in a tent," I scoffed, as I gazed around Bridget McQuire's team's magnificent pyramid set. "Andy Mikita's directing on the next sound stage," replied Wood. "He has a surprise." I bounced off round the corner full of anticipation — and there it was. A honking great tent, complete with a floor cushion reserved for the

newest Abydonian elder, and a serving vessel for her son! And yes, I did get to wear a voluminous costume, which incidentally was made out of the same canvas material as the tent...

Above: Let's go home.

Mr Wood did however have some more pressing issues to address with this very special episode: "At the end, I wanted to leave the viewer with a very powerful image. We're back on the barren planet that we originally landed on, so the ending is very symbolic. The new SG-1 walking away towards the Stargate is very much a 'walking into the sunset' shot, that works as a final ending, or as a bridge into a TV movie, or a theatrical movie, or another season.

"The episode was a chance to do bigger, sweeping movements with the camera, and more elaborate crane shots — to make it feel more like a movie," Wood concludes. "Our episodes had been getting bigger and wider all year, and I wanted to do this one so that it wouldn't be apparent where the episode ends and the movie begins, had things panned out that way." Things didn't pan out that way in the end of course... onwards to season seven! ⋋

Colonel Jack O'Neill

"We've stayed ahead of the game only because we didn't bite off more than we could chew... normally."

Colonel Jack O'Neill (the one with two 'L's — the other one apparently doesn't have a sense of humour) has had quite a time over the past two years. What with new super-bugs, new super foes, more false gods than you can shake a staff weapon at and the loss (well nearly) of two good friends, it's enough to keep the smile off his face.

"I suppose the Colonel has had quite a time," muses Mr Anderson. "Remind me what happened again?" In common with his fictional *Stargate* counterpart, the actor can suffer from selective memory loss, which seems to worsen when asked to recount some details from the past two seasons. "Can't I tell you about my new bike?" he asks. "Or what about my random thoughts I'm thinking of publishing — as if anyone will read them." Assurances that at least one poor soul would eagerly pore over his collected ramblings accompany a stern admonishment that there must be one or two incidents that stick in his notoriously vague mind. "What?" he insists. "Here, have a look at these pictures of my daughter." It's impossible to resist the teasing twinkle in Anderson's eye as he steers, nay, railroads the conversation towards his very favourite subject.

"She's my angel," he smiles, referring to the very beautiful, very self-assured young lady in the photos. "Wylie is my reason for living. I can put up with the 5.30am starts and the rigours of working twelve hours a day knowing that I'll be with her at the end of the week. Our directors are usually really good at getting me wrapped reasonably early on Fridays, so that I can dash straight to the airport and be on my way to her. It's really important for me to be there to enjoy and observe, and be a part of this stage of her development. Obviously, I want to be with her throughout her developing years, but now is a particularly special time." Anderson is delighted that his daughter has inherited his family's love and appreciation of all kinds of music. "She loves the classical stuff, in fact one of her favourite videos is set to Bach, and she's definitely into jazz." That's a trait Wylie shares with her father and grandfather.

Apparently Miss Anderson is a bit of a daredevil on skis, although this is one area where Daddy has been happy to take a bit of a back seat.

"We went on our first father/daughter skiing trip not too long ago and I did want to teach her personally but, well, you know what it's like. I wanted her to learn the basics properly — but she wanted to fly down the slopes like Daddy." Attempting an unsuccessful nonchalance about being wrapped around her little finger, Anderson states "Wylie and I came to a mutual decision that it was best for her to go into ski school for a couple of hours, and then join me later. We were set after that."

Anderson's memory also improves when talking about the other project dear to his heart — the conservation of our Earth's natural resources and wildlife: "A friend runs Earth River Expeditions, and he invited me to be part of a documentary film group whose intention is to raise awareness of the plight of the great rivers of the world. We want to educate the outside world as to how to preserve these amazing resources, and highlight what could happen if the rivers are over-developed by big businesses. It's a work in progress, but we hope to eventually see it shown on the Discovery Channel or National Geographic."

In between running his own family and running rivers, Anderson has found time to devote the odd hour or ten to running with the *Stargate* franchise. By the start of season six, the show had departed from Showtime and arrived all guns blazing on the SCI FI Channel — a move Anderson, as executive producer, took in his stride. Shrugging he says, "I was totally OK with the change of network and am very happy to be supported by the SCI FI Channel. The Powers

That Be worked out the sums, and it looked good for all the parties concerned, so in a financial and creative sense it would have been foolish to go any other way."

Despite his apparent amnesia, the actor offers a few opinions on the way *Stargate SG-1* has progressed. "Obviously, Michael Shanks's departure at the end of season five signalled a time of transition for us all. Michael had expressed some concerns about his involvement — or his perceived lack of it — in the show, and indicated that he wanted to move on. Michael has always been a very valued member of our group, so the wheels were put in motion to accommodate his wishes. He knew that he could return at any time, and in fact has done so several times throughout our sixth season. He is a very solid actor. He's also flexible enough to deal with my bursts of spontaneity, so I always have good moments with him."

Like the character he portrays, Anderson is pragmatic about the arrival of new cast regular Corin Nemec. "People move on and we needed to fill a gap. Corin Nemec coming in was a result of that. I've heard that some discontent was voiced by Daniel Jackson supporters, but the introduction of the Jonas character was part of the natural evolution of the show. And he's doing a good job. Sure, it must be difficult coming into an established group that shares the amount of history we do but, we're a pretty friendly bunch and there are worse places to be."

Talk of 'places to be' brings us round to where the actor feels he wants to be in the not too distant future. "Well, I'll stop short of saying I'm going to retire outright, but I will be taking steps to make sure that I ease back on work a lot more, so I can spend time with my little girl. This may mean I spend less time in Vancouver and more in California. We're currently trying to figure out how to make that happen — but it will happen. I feel like I'm somewhat ready to start enjoying what I've worked fairly hard to achieve! As for the longer term... who knows. Having spent such a large part of my life living within the *Stargate* universe, I admit that I am looking forward to experiencing different horizons. It will be quite a transition and will, no doubt, be fraught with new challenges, but on the whole, I'm pleasantly anticipating that time."

As for the very irreverent Colonel, Anderson says, "At this juncture, I have no idea what's in store for O'Neill, or where he is headed. But I'm sure he'll get to wherever he's going in his usual straightforward, nonchalant way!" ⅄

Major Sam Carter

"You do have a penchant for pulling brilliant ideas out of your butt... head... when we need them."

In terms of character, Major Sam Carter has to be one of the strongest women in the world. Time and time again she has fought for what she believes, against the Goa'uld, against the shadowy figures within her country's government and against prejudice directed towards her simply because she's female. She's done it with grace, style and dignity, and Amanda Tapping is thrilled with the outcome: "It's been well documented that from the start I wanted to show how strong Sam was, without sacrificing any of her femininity. The more I've talked with people who watch and enjoy the show, the more I realise how important it is that women and men understand what a powerful force any individual can be without resorting to clichéd stereotypes. I love that people seem to be responding to that message. Both Teryl [Rothery] and I have had messages from people of all ages who tell us how great it is to see women who get the job done without having to become 'one of the boys'. It's very fulfilling."

Away from *Stargate SG-1*, Tapping has been spreading the good word amongst those interested in entering her profession: "I was asked to be a guest speaker at a Women in Film Flash Forward seminar," she says, "which encourages young film-makers, actors, writers, producers and the like to pitch projects, and offers examples of how to take their careers forward to the next level. I don't consider myself an expert by any means, but it was great just to sit and talk about acting, and the kind of control you have, and the kind you don't have. It was good simply to share our experiences because, in this business, there are so many factors stacked against us. You know: how you look, how tall you are, what age you are. I'm a firm believer that from the moment you walk into an audition room, it should all be about support. I believe that in the work I do here, and I hope that comes across when Sam shows her solidarity for the members of SG-1 and the rest of her colleagues at the SGC."

The actress takes her job, and her role as an ambassador, very seriously, but she's also a firm believer in the power of humour, and so undertakes these tasks in the most light-hearted way possible. Though quite often she doesn't really have much choice in the matter, particularly when it comes to the all-action gung-ho stuff, as Ms

Tapping has a lot less control over her limbs and laughter than her *Stargate* alter-ego. Known for her ability to trip over thin air, Tapping gives us a glimpse of her inability to get head, hands, feet and body working at the same time. Punctuation has been added but, as anyone who has ever had the good fortune to meet this woman will know, there was a lot of gesticulation involved and she hardly drew a breath...

Diary of a would-be Stunt Woman
By Amanda Tapping

Yeah! 'Smoke and Mirrors'! O'Neill is charged with murder and Sam goes off to the NID. I got to wear more normal clothes, sort of *Men In Black* stuff, and a nice pretty skirt. See — it's all about the wardrobe with me! But — what's *really* important about this episode is that I actually, for the first time ever in the history of six years of *Stargate*, got a stunt operator. I probably should have gotten some in the past because of the outrageous things I've done. You should see some of the ridiculous things I've flung myself at! But with this one I went up to our assistant director and said, "I'm charging down concrete steps, leaping over a wall and a building is exploding behind me. I'm pretty sure that's a stunt." So we (that's Peter Flemming, who played Barrett, and I) practiced. We run to the end of this wall and we have to do a leap. Now, there is a mat in one position, and there are cameras positioned all around it and there's this whole 'Don't hit the camera, leap over here, land on this big fluffy mat' vibe. But every time we rehearsed it, as soon as I got close to the wall, I'd do this little gymnast-style hop, skip and leap. And people were like, "Amanda — just run and leap. Run, and leap.

What's with the gymnast thing?" So I keep landing on the mat and I'd spring up and go, "Whoo Hoo! Six point four from the Russian judge!" which I thought was quite funny, but the crew were getting nervous: "She's gotta get this right. She *has* to get it." I mean, God bless the crew. I think they really like me, but they also know that I'm *completely* uncoordinated and therefore a great source of entertainment on a daily basis.

Anyway, I'm scared. I have to run down these concrete steps and they weren't built to code if you know what I mean, they're too narrow, but I can't back out because it's this huge shot and the whole neighbourhood has turned out. The spectators are all going, "Wow! They're going to blow up this house!" and though we won't *actually* blow it up, there is going to be a big explosion, which has taken all day to set up.

So — it's the last stunt of the day. The crew is trying to reassure me: "No worries, Amanda!" One of the stunt guys has grabbed hold of the end of the mat, to hold it up so that when I land I don't come sliding off the end. However on the last rehearsal I come flying at him, I land... and he literally punches me in the face because he's holding the mat and I collide with his fist. Then I'm holding my nose going "Oh crap" and he's all apologetic, saying "I was trying to help you" and I'm like "No! No! I'm an accident waiting to happen!" I then remember I have a gun in my hand, and that's something *else* I have to contend with.

Finally, we're all set to shoot. Go! I'm running down the stairs, everyone is watching. There's five cameras rolling — it's just the huge-est thing. I do the leap. I'm all good. I realise the camera is in front of me so I have to tuck in. I do it, land... and as I land... I smash myself in the face with my gun! I'm lying there stunned and I can feel the heat of the explosion and I'm like "Oh Boy!" I touch my face, which is all wet, and I thought it was blood. Turned out it wasn't — it was just snot. But my eyes are watering because I smashed myself on the nose.

Everyone is going, "Wow. That was fantastic!" I turned to Jack from craft service and said, "You know, just *once* I would like to do a stunt where I didn't incur some sort of injury." Then Dan Shea, our stunt co-ordinator and big wrench carrier comes up and says, "I've never worked with an actress who does her own stunts." I say, "Ya think I should stop?" and he replies, "Yeah. Amanda, God is sending you messages." You know what? I think next time, I'll listen. ⋏

Teal'c

> "I have heard of a place where people do battle... in a ring of jello."

Teal'c has certainly had his fair share of ups and downs during *Stargate*'s past two seasons. He's had the symbiote literally ripped out of him a couple of times; been treated like the Shol'va he was by his son; he's admitted his love for *Star Wars*; found a new friend and lost a best buddy. "Yeah!" laughs Christopher Judge, "you could say that it has been a bit of roller-coaster ride, and it's been a complete blast!"

The first of the character's near-death experiences occurred after his old mate and god, Apophis, brainwashed him into thinking the humans were a bunch of infidels who had to be crushed once more. Luckily, Teal'c's other old friend and mentor was on hand to remove his Goa'uld symbiote, and let Teal'c decide which team to bat for. "'Threshold' was a pretty intense episode and a lot of fun to do," says Judge. "But they did have me almost naked in the snow, which I think was just a way of getting back at me for all the jokes I've played on people over the years," he moans.

With characteristic aplomb, Judge goes on, "Did you see that episode, though? I looked pretty fit, huh? I'd been working out all hiatus and even if I do say so myself, I think I was looking pretty good!" Remarks that he might have looked passing fit, in a dim light, if one was wearing sunglasses or had eye strain are met with a shout of laughter. "Hey! If you don't mind, I should point out that I've had fan mail telling me how good I looked!"

Leaving his appearance aside, Judge is quick to praise the performances of his fellow actors. "Tony Amendola is the best. You know, he's so wise, so giving, so gracious and so like the character... apart from the age thing," he grins. "Even the mischievous streak is there. There's a scene in 'Threshold' where Bra'tac is giving Teal'c a bit of a lecture, and then hits him out of the blue. The surprise on my face is real. It's in the script that I get hit, but I sure didn't know when it was coming!

"Tony's the same away from the studio," Judge continues. "We often hang out together as a group when he's in town, and you can always tell where he is in a room because of the laughter. You'll see him in what looks like a serious conversation and as he walks away,

he'll deliver some line or comment that is totally unexpected, that'll leave the other person in hysterics. I just love him."

Judge also has a great relationship with Neil Denis, the young man who plays his son Rya'c: "I have three kids of my own and am thoroughly enjoying them growing up, as I am with Neil. He was just the sweetest kid when we first met, and now is a fine young man. He always was a good kid and has definitely grown into a son Teal'c can be proud of. Now, if only I can do that sort of job with my own..." (Having met all three of Judge's children I can truly say they are a credit to their Dad.)

In keeping with Judge's own jovial character, the producers and writers have made Teal'c progressively lighter as the seasons have progressed. It's a move the actor welcomes with open arms: "He's becoming a lot less reserved, which is something I've been pushing for. I've always said that I wanted to see Teal'c assimilate more into human culture. After all he comes from human stock, so it makes perfect sense to me that after a few years he would begin to lean more toward that side. I love that he can now get some of the jokes and humorous references, and can respond in kind.

"For example," the actor goes on, visibly warming to his theme, "there's a gag in 'The Other Guys', when O'Neill and Teal'c are captured and O'Neill has just finished one of his rants. He turns to Teal'c and asks, 'Whaddya think?' and I can't remember the exact line, but Teal'c tells him his timing needs work. I was supposed to deliver that with a straight face, but of course couldn't. It tickled me that Teal'c would respond that way, and the look on Rick's face was absolutely priceless. It took umpteen takes before either of us could do it straight."

Although there has been a lot of laughter on and off the set, Judge admits that it was quite a wrench to lose Michael Shanks as a regular cast member. But all is not gloom and doom. "I do miss seeing him every day at work," he says, "but we hang out more at night and at the weekends than ever. I also did an episode of *Andromeda* with him where I played his brother ship — or sister ship — depending on how you want to look at it. That was great, getting to work with Michael in a completely different environment."

Talk of different environments brings us round to what Mr Judge does to keep himself out of mischief when he does have time off from work, besides torturing small balls on the golf course that is. "Well, I've always been a keen photographer," the actor adds, "so I've been honing that craft. I really want to do stuff for the big glossies, *Maxim*, *Vogue* — publications like that. I have a studio and am building up my portfolio. My girlfriend Gianna is an actress, and also a fantastic make-up artist and we're hoping to develop... no pun intended... a business offering professional photographic services. I've taken some really cool shots of some of the cast here. Some really sexy shots of Amanda and Teryl." Rumbling with laughter Judge admits, "Jan Newman, our make-up supervisor, doesn't like them because they look a little *too* glamorous if you get my drift."

Back in the *Stargate* universe, Judge is content with the way things have gone in season six. "I had a great time writing 'The Changeling'. It was such a collaborative experience that I'm looking forward to the next time." Asked if there was anything that drove him bananas and made him hang his head in frustration he replies, "You mean apart from the cast, the crew and the caterers? No! Not one thing. Everyone pulled out all the stops to make this one hell of a production. I'm extremely proud of the finished article, and of them."

Judge is delighted that the SCI FI Channel has had the good sense to want *Stargate SG-1* to continue for a further year at least. "Not just because it means I can pay off my debts," he winks. "I think there are more facets of Teal'c to reveal. There is so much more to develop with regard to the relationships between the characters, and there are many more great stories to tell. I'm really looking forward to being a part of that." λ

Dr Daniel Jackson

"Maybe I did some good now and again, but nothing I've ever done seems to have changed anything."

For six years archaeologist, anthropologist, best friend and work-mate Daniel Jackson has been the voice of reason at the SGC. He's coaxed, persuaded and cajoled his SG-1 team mates, his boss, General Hammond, the government, the Goa'uld and indeed anyone who would listen, that much more can be achieved by studying other cultures to learn about them, rather than simply blasting a way into any given situation. His message hasn't been lost on the show's audience either. Masses of letters and e-mails arrive at the Bridge Studios every day, thanking the actor for the positive influence he's had on their lives. "It's interesting," says Michael Shanks, "because I'm only now beginning to learn what impact the character has on the world out-side the studio. He's a character that is based around the best and most idealistic of intentions. Certainly, there are things about Daniel that are strong qualities that we, as 'good' individuals, cherish. That's why I like the character so much! When I hear that Daniel's attitude toward life and the many challenges it offers has had an impact on somebody else's 'real' life — that's totally overwhelming. It's humbling. I'm not sure it's deserved but, I always say, 'If you can help someone, then do it.'"

Even though he was used to a certain amount of mail appearing on a daily basis, Shanks was completely nonplussed by the sheer vol-ume of correspondence that deluged the studio, the programme mak-ers and executives when he decided to leave the show. The actor was amazed at the amount of personal messages of support he received, and was very touched by the sentiments expressed. "It was very flat-tering and a great barometer to indicate the character's influence in the series," he says. "That level of support certainly re-affirmed, in my mind, how valued Daniel really was. I had been feeling somewhat undervalued at that time. I felt that certain expectations hadn't been met and certain personal goals had not been achieved, so it was very flattering to receive these acknowledgments. I can't say this was my sole reason for wanting to return to the show on a regular basis for sea-son seven, but it certainly helped focus my mind on where I wanted to be, and what I wanted to do."

Although Shanks worked on other projects during his time away from *Stargate SG-1*, he never left the show completely. "I came back

to do several episodes in season six, and realised how much I missed everybody and the environment. I had such a great time and everyone was so welcoming and delighted to see me, it dawned on me that I *did* want to return as a regular cast member once more. I am really happy to be coming back and am extremely grateful to our producers and to the powers at SCI FI for backing my return. We have the best of relationships, and I'm really looking forward to stepping through the Gate, renewed and refreshed."

During his sabbatical from Stargate Command, Shanks got to travel and see a bit of *this* world, starting at the opposite end of Canada. "I went to Toronto, to do a movie called *All Around the Town*. I did that with Nastassia Kinski. I played a good guy in that one. He's a psychologist whose client is a girl with multiple personalities. She's accused of murder, and he tries to separate the various personas to figure out which one of them is responsible for her actions. It was really interesting because it was such a different kind of role for me to play. It was also fun, if a little daunting to work on a completely different set, with a brand new group of people. After a number of years, or in the case of *Stargate*, almost immediately, you get very comfortable on 'your' set, so it was exciting if a little nerve-wracking to become 'the newbie' on someone else's ground."

Shanks then crossed the Atlantic to attend his first European convention. "I had a blast!" he smiles. "Living in a kind of vacuum up in Vancouver, and having never really attended this kind of thing previously, I had no idea of the level of interest, or sheer *enthusiasm*, of the British and European fans. They were great and I plan to do a lot more — if they invite me." The actor was also looking forward to travelling to the Indian sub-continent. "I've been asked to do a movie called *Children of the Monsoon*, which means I may have to go to India for a month. I can't wait. It's a place I've always wanted to visit." Shanks returned to Canada briefly to appear in an episode of *Andromeda*, alongside girlfriend Lexa Doig, and fellow guest star Christopher Judge. "That was a hoot!" Shanks recalls. "It was less like work, and more like hanging out at home with some good friends. Obviously I've gotten to know the guys over at *Andromeda* partially through Lexa, and because I'd done an episode previously. This one was a lot of fun with lots of action, fighting, guns and whatnot." Shanks enjoyed one last far-flung adventure before returning to off-world duties. "I'd always wanted to go to South Africa, because Michael Greenburg kept telling me how wonderful it was, plus his wife Nikki is from there and *she* told me how beautiful it was too. Fortunately, I was asked to do a movie down there, and it was quite an experience. It's called *Sumuru*, and I play a soldier of fortune who travels to the last Earth colony to try to rescue the last remaining people before they become extinct. I was surrounded by 120 scantily clad South African models, which was *highly* entertaining. But please don't tell my girlfriend."

Safely ensconced in *Stargate* once again, Shanks is more than ready to meet the challenges of the forthcoming seventh year. "Richard Dean Anderson has decided to spend more time with his daughter, and devote more of his energies in that direction. One of the results of his decision is that all the other characters will have the opportunity to do a bit more. This increased responsibility and chance to get involved a lot more was another reason why I wanted to come back. Yes, it does mean that we will see Daniel Jackson on screen more, but I'm also going to be involved in other facets of the film-making process." Shanks successfully directed the episode 'Double Jeopardy' in season four, and now reveals "I'm going to be writing an episode. Chris Judge had such a great time; I thought I'd follow in his footsteps and throw my ideas into the pot too. It'll be interesting to go through the process of how something gets from my mind to the screen. It'll be a real learning curve and I can't wait to see how it pans out!" ⅄

Jonas Quinn

"He's a nerd, sir. He and Daniel got on great."

Jonas Quinn has travelled a few million miles since he first jumped through the Stargate at the end of season five. Corin Nemec's journey to the production also involved racking up the miles, but by more conventional means. "I was living down in San Antonio, Texas and had flown up to Vancouver to do an episode of *Smallville*," says the actor. "After I'd flown back home, I heard about the offer of the role in *Stargate*, so flew right back again. A lot of travelling but, boy, was it worth it."

Jonas arrives on Earth, a virtual refugee, and a fugitive from his own people, who are not best pleased that he goes against their version of events in order to restore Daniel Jackson's good name. It doesn't help that he 'procures' a quantity of naquadria, a source of super-fuel, for the humans as well. "Yeah! Well, what had to be done had to be done," says Nemec, "and Jonas is a man of integrity and his word. It would be completely against his nature to allow Daniel to sacrifice his reputation for basically a bunch of warmongers. Jonas is definitely one of the good guys."

Nemec has been in the acting business for over fifteen years, and feels privileged to be still enjoying himself: "I started acting professionally when I was twelve. I did little bits and pieces, but then the first major production I appeared in was *Tucker*, directed by Francis Ford Coppola. I played the part of Noble Tucker when I was just thirteen, so to be in the industry and still be having a great time after so long is a blessing. A lot of people get jaded, which surprises me, but I look forward to the challenge that each new day brings."

Nemec believes this perennially positive attitude toward the industry is in part due to the influence of his parents: "When I decided to go into acting, it was because it seemed the right thing to do. Both my parents are artists. I was raised to be an artist, but I didn't know which direction to take. Then I found acting and got involved in a theatre company, and it just seemed the perfect way for me to go, so off I went!"

Nemec is still involved with the American Repertory Company in Los Angeles, where he has worked for the past six years, but whether it be theatre or film, "for me it's all about the creative process. The enjoyment of creating a piece of 'life' that doesn't exist

in reality. When it's put on stage, or filmed, edited together and put on screen, it becomes a slice of life. It becomes a kind of reality that people enjoy."

Although up for any kind of performance art, the actor prefers film: "With film, I get to become a character that is different from my reality as Corin Nemec. But the bizarre thing about film — which you don't get with theatre — is that I get to view back this alternate reality. It's like being able to re-run your dream in the morning when you wake up, but this time you get to watch it. There's physical evidence of you living this other life, playing this other character, which is not you. Obviously there are aspects of you in it, but in a different reality."

Nemec says this revelation came to him when he went to see a film on which his father worked. "My dad [Joe Nemec III] had done the art direction on the movie *The Goonies*. He designed the big pirate ship and the interior of the cave. He told me that when I saw this movie, I was going to flip. He was right!

"Watching it was what triggered me wanting to be an actor. I thought, 'These guys get to do this incredible story: get chased by bad guys and run through all these caves, go down water slides and fight with pirates — but it's not *real*. I mean, I'd been on sets from a young age and I 'knew' it wasn't real. I had knowledge of the process that went into making it look real, but my main thought was that the actors get to *pretend* — and get paid! That's what triggered it all off for me. And up to and including this day, being involved in this business, and the aesthetic process, has to be one of the most rewarding careers, no matter what you do."

Whilst Nemec's acting journey began on a fantasy adventure platform, he's been happy to cross genres as and when required. "I've been fortunate to have had quite a variety of roles," he grins. "I played the lead in *Parker Lewis Can't Lose* for many years, and between that show and now I've appeared in the Stephen King miniseries *The Stand, Drop Zone* with Wesley Snipes and *Operation Dumbo Drop*, which was a very light-hearted comedy I enjoyed doing very much."

Looking perplexed for a moment he muses, "The funny thing is that in the last four or five years, I've ended up playing the bad guy. It started after I did *The Stand*, because in that I played a really dodgy character, and after that people saw me in a different light. It's kind of carried on from there. The last bad guy I played was killed, so I'm kinda hoping that's the death of the bad guys for a while!"

In order to take his mind away from the stresses of playing a role — good or bad — Nemec will immerse himself in a book, or listen to some soothing sounds. "I'm very like Jonas in that I'm always reading," he says. "I love to read, although I don't read fiction. It's sort of a rule I made for myself, because I like to understand what is real. It's particularly important when I'm so heavily involved in a process that deals so much with fictional, unreal situations.

"Music-wise I really enjoy East Indian music, especially the stuff that doesn't have any singing," Nemec continues. "It's not that I dislike the singing, but just the traditional sounds are what I particularly like. I'm also into reggae dub in a big way. Over the past year I've been sort of getting into more mainstream rock. There's some amazing music out there, and a lot of the singers have some pretty strong points of view in the right direction. On the whole though, I'm into world music, and will go into the Virgin Megastore and walk straight to the International section. I don't mind which country it is. It can be African, South American, Asian, European. If the cover looks good, I buy it, take it home and check it out. I like finding out about the world through music."

Nemec also like to find out about the world through *Stargate* fans, and is hoping to meet as many as possible in Vancouver, and farther afield: "Taking the opportunity to communicate with the people who watch your show, and who appreciate what you're doing, is of tremendous importance to me. I think I'll really enjoy it." You can bet the fans will enjoy it too. ⅄

Recurring Characters

Brad Wright

"Our intention is to continue to introduce new and exciting characters that will become part of our on-going mythology."

S
easons five and six of *Stargate SG-1* have continued to add to the show's rich and varied roster of recurring characters. Sadly, there's simply too many to include them all. However, here's the latest from some of the most familiar… Whilst he may not exactly rule the SGC with a rod of iron, **General Hammond** certainly displays an iron will when it comes to protecting his troops and the integrity of the Stargate programme. For six years, the good general has had to contend with everything from alien probes, to alienating a faction of the US government: he'll do anything to keep the facility at Cheyenne Mountain safe from marauders, in human guise or otherwise.

Actor Don S. Davis is proud to have been given the opportunity to portray such a commendable character. "I've always said that my previous military experience has stood me in good stead when it comes to thinking through some of the decisions that Hammond has had to make," he says. "The welfare of the men and women under his command has always been paramount in his mind. One of the things I hope I've been able to show is that here is a man who, when faced with a decision to send his people to places from where they might not return, will do it only when there is no other course of action for him to take." That said, Davis is also proud of the way the General knows when to step back, and hold fire: "There have been times when Hammond has had to reluctantly decide against military intervention, even for a rescue attempt, simply because it would mean putting yet more lives in danger. Every one of his people is precious to him but, sometimes, he has had to let go — always reluctantly, and always with regret. I hope I've been able to show that he has kept his integrity, without losing his humanity."

The actor's fondness for SG-1 extends beyond the Stargate: "One of the many blessings I've received through being involved with this show is the gift of friendship. I am as close to some of my co-workers as I am to members of my family. In fact, they are like members of my family. One of the biggest testaments to that is the time we spend together away from the studios. We often eat dinner together when we leave work for the night — Teryl Rothery does a mean pot roast — and at the weekends we'll often hang out at Chris Judge's movie star

home, or have a barbecue at Amanda Tapping's place. I've just moved house recently, so am looking forward to extending some homespun hospitality of my own real soon!"

When he's not entertaining the troops (so to speak), Davis is happiest in solitary pursuits and indulges his passion for drawing, painting and sculpting as much as possible. "I've recently returned from France, where I spent the most glorious time just wandering round some private galleries and truly awe-inspiring temples like the Louvre," he sighs. "I never, ever tire of absorbing the work of the great masters. For me, immersion in their work is like balm to my soul. I love soft, round, sensual forms and colour: the more vibrant and striking the better. I also have a very soft spot for balls! You know, spheres. I have the most wonderful collection of them scattered inside and outside my home. I have them in wood, stone, plastic, paper and glass. I just love their mystery; the infinite possibilities contained within that shape. I think there is something inherently mystical about a perfect circle." Ah! No wonder he's always staring at the Stargate...

With possibilities for season seven wide open, Davis has one wish for General Hammond in the future. "Everyone thinks of him as stern and straight laced — kind of fuddy-duddy really," he says. "What I'd like to see is an episode where Hammond becomes some alien's love slave!" The producers have promised us a wealth of new experiences next year. Perhaps Davis will get his wish...

Steadfastly keeping the bodies and minds of her SG teammates together, **Janet Fraiser** has been exactly the sort of doctor anyone would order when the best kind of bedside manner is required. Stubborn, strong and not above pulling rank — if not height — over her wayward charges, Fraiser has been far more than a medic, particularly with regard to SG-1. "Although professionalism dictates that Janet gives her all for every patient she treats, I think it's fair to say she has a particularly soft spot for the guys in SG-1," Teryl Rothery says. "She raises a child with Sam Carter for a start, and is quite possibly the only person who can make Jack O'Neill lie still and take his medicine! Not that he does it for long, of course, but perhaps a millisecond more than he would do for anyone else... I think a great deal of love and respect has grown between the good doctor and SG-1 over the years.

"One of the neat things that has been happening throughout season five, and certainly in season six, is that we do get to see Janet's relationships with the other SG-1 guys developing," Rothery continues. "In 'Smoke and

Mirrors', for example, we all band together to help O'Neill: three of us — Fraiser, Teal'c and Jonas — work at the base to do that. We had some great little scenes, and it was so nice to get to work with the 'boys' for a change."

Whilst Fraiser has been working with the boys quite a bit, there doesn't seem to be a lot happening in her love life. Sighing dramatically the actress shrugs, "No! She's still celibate, that girl. I keep saying to Brad Wright and some of the other producers, 'I don't know why you don't just approach Patrick Stewart and have him guest star — you know what I'm saying? It would be fabulous. Fraiser goes off world. She meets this 'being' or 'Statesperson', and they just hit it off!' I've been working on it, but they don't seem to be jumping at that storyline…"

Away from *Stargate*, Rothery's characters have been getting more than their fair share of lurve, however: "I did a guest star spot on *Jeremiah* where I got to play Luke Perry's mom in flashback. So I have a loving husband and family in that one. Then I did a guest spot on a show called *Glory Days*, playing a very nasty character who is having an affair, and ends up shooting her lover by mistake. I loved having the opportunity to play someone that nasty!" Back in her true Ms Nice mode, Rothery made a triumphant return to live theatre, appearing in the children's musical *Merlin*. "I had a blast!" she confirms. "I was a little nervous after concentrating on work in television and films, but I loved the rehearsal process and the buzz of being 'live'. It was great to get back to my performing roots."

So, what is in store for the medical marvel in *Stargate*'s seventh season? This little message from the lady herself might give a clue…

A Few Words...
By Teryl Rothery

The lovely Ms Thomasina Gibson has asked me to write a few words for her new book. Given the fact that her deadline is fast approaching as I write this, and my schedule keeps getting more and more hectic with each passing day, it will in fact be just a *very* few words!

We are now filming the seventh season of *Stargate*, and that means it will soon be time for me to… oops, nearly gave the game away. Just let me say 'thank you' to each and every one of you for supporting the show all these years. I also want to say thank you for embracing the character of Dr Janet Fraiser almost as much as I have. It will be a sad moment when, one day, we have to say goodbye, but I can honestly say that this role will always remain one of my favourites! My heartfelt thanks again… Always, Teryl Rothery.

In *Stargate SG-1*, Master **Bra'tac** seems to devote his life to encouraging rebellious behaviour amongst far-flung Jaffa. On this planet however, actor Tony Amendola seems to spend a lot of his time flying off to far-flung places to enjoy the fruits of a very lively and varied career. Television appearances have included guest star spots on *Alias*, *Charmed* and *The Practice*. He achieved a life-long dream by playing the title role in a theatre production of *Cyrano* and, when we spoke, had just returned from Bulgaria, where he was shooting a fantasy movie. Not bad for a man of 130-odd years! Fortunately, six years on, Amendola is still keen to come back to mentor Teal'c and pester O'Neill. "It's funny because when I first auditioned for the part of Bra'tac, it seemed like it was going to be just another job," Amendola recalls. "But then I fell in love with the character and one thing led to another, and I'm delighted to still be here fighting the Goa'uld and making friends with the Tau'ri."

Even with a résumé as long as a staff weapon, Amendola insists that life on *Stargate SG-1* is a particular pleasure. "You know, I'm always saying how wonderful it is to be part of *Stargate*, but it really is true. They go out of their way to make things happen for you. The best example of that is when Brad Wright switched the filming schedules for 'Allegiance' around, just to accommodate me, because I was still play-

Bra'tac's Jaffa Warrior Pesto

2 cups pure grown Chulakian fresh basil
3 or 4 cloves of Rebel Jaffa style Goa'uld garlic
Half a cup of peace-nurturing Galaxy union imported Tok'ra olive oil
3 or 4 tablespoons of fresh grated Prim'ta Parmesan
2oz Zat-toasted pine-nuts or walnuts
Salt and pepper to suit your species

Combine in an Earth blender or food processor the fresh basil, garlic and a little olive oil, and make a smooth paste. Gradually add the Parmesan cheese and the rest of the olive oil and then toasted nuts, and continue to seek a paste with as few lumps as possible.
Practice Kel No Reem; meditate on your favourite warrior pesto dish.
Respectful serving suggestions include, spread over Prim'ta pasta garnished with a fresh spring of the Chulak basil and a very small Cheyenne mountain of toasted nuts or, as a garnish, in Stargate soups of any kind. Or perhaps a Rebel Jaffa omelette would be to your taste. It is one of Teal'c and my favourites. As we say on Chulak: Unob pptet'a! — Bon Appetit!
Master Bra'tac.

ing in *Cyrano* at the time. That is something that does not happen often in this business, I can tell you. I am touched and forever grateful."

Bra'tac can often appear austere and forbidding, but there is a distinctly mischievous side to the old master: just think of the taunts he throws toward Teal'c in 'Threshold', and he's never short of the odd quip for Jack O'Neill. Bra'tac's wry sense of humour is a trait shared by Mr Amendola. Asked to contribute a little something for this book, he laughed, "Well, you know, Jaffa warriors do not live on Kel No Reem alone. They do need physical sustenance to keep them fit and strong. Perhaps I could let you in on Bra'tac's secret passion… it's cooking. He's quite the gourmet!" So for your edification and delight (written with help from chef's assistant Tony Amendola), look out for a little offering from the master…

Major Paul Davis is a highly principled, dedicated man who often has the unenviable job of playing Devil's Advocate when it comes to matters pertaining to the Stargate programme. Davis does, however, have a great deal of respect for his colleagues at the SGC, and though he is technically there to provide liaison between the Pentagon and Hammond, he has joined forces with SG-1, actually working with Major Carter on one notable occasion to rescue Teal'c. Actor Colin Cunningham is the classic 'California Boy', and was raised in LA. He first appeared on stage as the result of a dare! He now writes, directs, produces and acts (and also plays a mean saxophone and guitar). In *Stargate*, Davis is the epitome of balanced professionalism. He does have a lighter side, however…

Memo from Major Davis
By 'Colin Cunningham'

I just wanted to say what a pleasure it is playing 'Colin Cunningham' when I'm not here on the base. Granted, when he's playing 'me', he gets to travel to distant parts of the galaxy and save the world. But on the other hand, when I'm 'him', I get to meet all sorts of cool fans and get to hang out with JR Bourne. Whoo Hoo!

Softly spoken, mild mannered and infinitely gentle, Tom McBeath couldn't be further from the sneaky, scheming character he portrays on *Stargate SG-1*. **Colonel Harry Maybourne** is a USAF officer and rogue NID agent whose life's ambition seems to be to thwart and torment Colonel Jack O'Neill at every possible opportunity. Ironically their hate/hate relationship, which manifests in highly entertaining bouts of mental, verbal and physical jousting, is a firm fan favourite. Referring to himself as a jobbing actor, McBeath (it's pronounced like the Shakespeare play) grins, "Mostly I play asses, jerks, perverts, guys that are a little bit on the edge. I don't know what it is about my past that's made me an expert on being an asshole, but I do them well! One of the challenges of playing that sort of role is to find the human qualities in them. I don't think there's a person on this Earth that's inherently evil, so it's my job to find qualities that the audience can identify with." With productions ranging from *Double Jeopardy* on film, to *Millennium* on TV, to an acclaimed production of *Art* on stage, McBeath's human

Production Design

"What can I say? Our production design team is a collaboration of genius."

When it comes to creating a world where no man — and just as often no Goa'uld — has gone before, *Stargate SG-1*'s production design team are in a class of their own. Each week, they weave their brand of practical magic around the ideas suggested by the show's writers, consistently conjuring up sets that feed the imaginations of both the actors called to work in and around them, and the viewers at home.

Richard Hudolin, production designer for the first five years of the show, has this explanation for the team's continuing success: "When you're working with the kind of budgetary and time restraints imposed on *Stargate SG-1*, it all comes down to the relationship between the crew, the writers and the producers — which is fantastic. It means a lot. They know we know our job, and they trust us to get on with it, and to do it well. They trust us so much that we've had occasions where Brad [Wright], Robert [Cooper] and John Smith have allowed us to expand even some of our most spectacular sets, because they know we can keep to budget. Sometimes they'll turn something into a two-parter, just because the set is so great and they want it to be in more than one episode!" Hudolin also admits the converse is true, but only on extreme occasions. "There have been very, very few times when the producers have cut something down because it will be more than a day's work for almost no screen time," he says. "But whatever their decision, you can be sure it's done with the production team's full collaboration and co-operation. Don't let anyone tell you any different!"

Having devoted five years to his favourite television show, Hudolin decided to venture into pastures new, leaving the team in the very capable hands of Bridget McGuire. She shares her former colleague's enthusiasm for the show, and given the amazing array of props and sets that have been built over the years, McGuire also advocates a bit of prudent recycling now and again. "I've been working as the art director for the last five years with Richard Hudolin, so I'm very familiar with the show, and the elements from the prior seasons," she explains. "It's great, because sometimes I can tell the guys, 'I remember that prop we used back in season two, episode three. Let's dust it off and use it again, only this time we'll do a few modifications so no one will recognise it.' It's wonderful to be able to pull out sets and items that have already been built, rather than make everything from scratch. It's a great resource."

Opposite page:
Designs for the torture room in 'Abyss' (top), and Anubis's new ship in 'Full Circle' (bottom).
Pages 132-133:
Production art from 'Changeling' and 'Cure', with 'Frozen' from design to final episode.

STARGATE SG-1
SEASON 6

Torture Room

Episode # 4 The Abyss
Drawn By: James Robbins

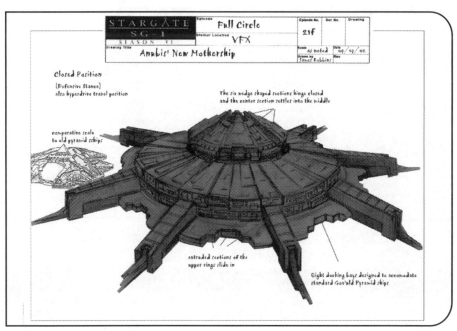

STARGATE
SG-1
SEASON VI

Episode: Full Circle

Station/ Location: VFX

Drawing Title: Anubis' New Mothership

Episode No.: 21f

Set No.

Drawing

Scale: As noted   Date: 09/19/02

Drawn by: James Robbins

Closed Position

(Defensive Stance)
also hyperdrive travel position

The six wedge shaped sections hinge closed
and the center section settles into the middle

comparative scale
to old pyramid ships

extruded sections of the
upper rings slide in

Eight docking bays designed to accomodate
standard Goa'uld pyramid ships

STARGATE SG-1
SEASON 4

Ancient Alien Woman frozen into Ice
- cloth cut away and pulled back to reveal her face

Episode 4: Upgrades
drawn by: James Robbins

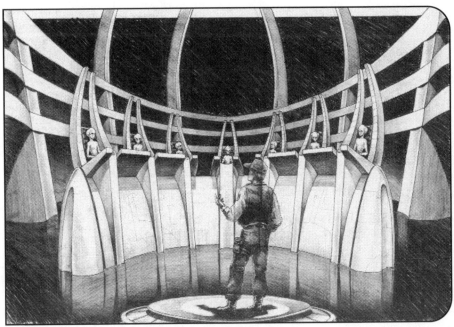

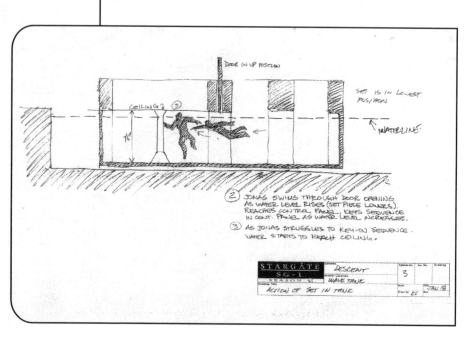

Handwritten annotations on drawing:
DOOR IN UP POSITION

CEILING 2 ③

SET IS IN LOWEST POSITION

WATERLINE

② JONAS SWIMS THROUGH DOOR OPENING AS WATER LEVEL RISES (SET PIECE LOWERS). REACHES CONTROL PANEL - KEYS SEQUENCE IN CONT. PANEL AS WATER LEVEL INCREASES.

③ AS JONAS STRUGGLES TO KEY-IN SEQUENCE. WATER STARTS TO REACH CEILING.

STARGÁTE SG-1 SEASON VI — DESCENT — WAVE TANK — 3

ACTION OF SET IN TANK — JAN 18

Pages 134-135:
Production designs
from 'Memento' (both
drawings on page
134), 'Paradise Lost'
and 'Red Sky'.
Above: *Design for*
the sinking set built in
a wave tank for
'Descent'.

McGuire reveals that though recycling works most of the time, there are occasions when something new has to be built to represent the old. "There's a scene in 'Abyss' where O'Neill wakes up inside the sarcophagus, but when we pulled out our poor old sarcophagus we found that it was in pretty rough shape," she admits. "We knew that the director wanted to so some pretty specific shots, so that gave us the perfect opportunity to rebuild it to his specifications."

One of the production design team's favourite sayings goes along the lines of 'the impossible we can do — miracles take a little longer'. This was amply demonstrated when the team had to design an underwater set for the episode 'Descent'. "SG-1 are on board a spaceship which seems to have been abandoned," McGuire recalls, "but then they discover that their friend Thor's brain is still active within the vessel, and they attempt to take it back with them. During that process, the ship crashes into the ocean, and a big part of the action is that the ship's corridors are being flooded with water. In order to facilitate this, we built a section of corridor that matched our set at the studios. It was then taken to the research wave pool at the University of British Columbia, and placed on a hydraulic lift so we could lower it into the water and simulate the flooding. It was a pretty ambitious project — nothing like that had ever been done on a television budget before!"

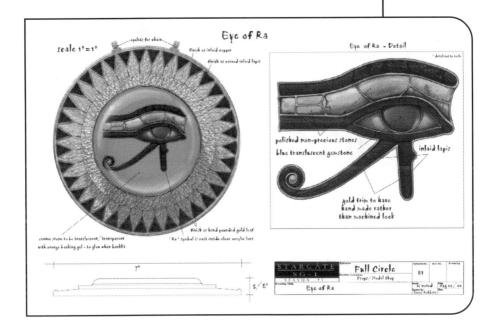

Having achieved the seeming impossible, McGuire admits it was a bit of a relief to have an easier episode on which to play. "'Nightwalkers' was great because it was an Earth-based episode," she sighs, "which meant we got to build regular sets like a sheriff's office, and a restaurant. It was a nice little break for us." Just as well, because McGuire's team then had their work cut out when it came to designing 'The Other Guys'. "Oh my gosh!" she exclaims. "We did fourteen different sets for a seven day shoot. Now that was *intense*."

Clearly gluttons for punishment, McGuire claims the highlight of the year for her and the rest of the production design crew was undoubtedly the creation, building and decoration of the sets for the season six finale: "The amount of intricate detail the guys managed to combine in one episode was incredible. 'Full Circle' really was one of the pinnacles for me. We just decided to pull out all the stops, and everybody really threw themselves into it, and had a ball. We thought, 'This may well be the last time we do anything like this again,' so we went all out. People really wanted to add their own little bits and pieces, their own special touches. Right up until moments before shooting, we were tweaking things to make it just so. The paintings were authentic and incredibly detailed. The props looked literally out of this world, and the whole thing looked truly amazing. I'm not ashamed to say we gave ourselves a little pat on the back for that!" ʎ

Above: An intricate design drawing for The Eye of Ra, as seen in 'Full Circle'.

Visual Effects

Michael Greenburg

"Our look just seems to be getting richer and bigger all the time with respect to SFX and VFX."

One of the most striking qualities of *Stargate SG-1* is the stunning visual effects produced under the auspices of master craftsman James Tichenor. Dedicated to producing groundbreaking effects without breaking the bank, Tichenor, the team at *Stargate SG-1* and their group of vendors continue to astound and delight all who watch the show. The effects team has been honoured with award nominations in previous years, but Tichenor is especially proud of the Emmy nominations they garnered for two very special episodes.

"We try to do the best job we can every single show, but two episodes that are particularly dear to my heart have to be the season five opener and the closer, 'Enemies' and 'Revelations',," he smiles. "Those were the ones we got the Emmy nominations for.

"'Enemies' was big in that it had a real broad range of different effects, lots of virtual sets and then the grand-daddy bugs, the soldier bugs and numerous versions of the Replicators. The episode was especially tricky because it was the third time we'd seen the Replicators, and we were continuing to up the ante in terms of what we could with them. We were trying to create more of a character for them. We also added newer bad guys into the mix, and then, of course, there was the final sequence, which was all shot with a hand-held camera. That was the first time we'd shot anything that dynamic in that particular way. Usually when you do a visual effects shot, you either lock the camera off so it doesn't move at all, or you have a fairly track-able move. This time though, we decided we wanted to go fully hand-held for this one sequence, just because it made it look a lot more immediate, exciting and dramatic. Fortunately, those who watch the show thought the same."

Twenty-two weeks after shooting 'Enemies', Tichenor was just as enthusiastic about developing new concepts in visual effects: "'Revelations' at the end of the year was particularly special to us. For a year and a half, as a kind of side project, we'd been researching and developing a computer generated [CG] character based on the Asgard, Thor. Brad [Wright] told me toward the end of the season that they were going to be doing an episode where we meet an Asgard scientist named Heimdall, who was Thor's buddy. We had got to a point where the testing with our CG character had succeeded well

Above: The CGI Replicators returned in 'Unnatural Selection'.

enough for me to go to Brad, and say, 'We want to try it out!'" Laughing about the lack of budget, Tichenor says, "The usual response we get is, 'Well, we can't afford that!' but in this particular instance, Image Engine, who did the effects on that episode, agreed to do it for about a third of the cost of producing the effects, because they wanted the experience and the credit of actually creating a fully walking, talking, acting CG character." To everyone's delight, the little alien worked spectacularly well.

Clearly enthralled, Tichenor proclaims, "It was really *neat*. It was very complicated but when you watch, it looks deceptively simple. This is because it comes across as just another character in the scene, which is exactly what everything — all the hard work — was going toward, you know? Creating that illusion — a walking, talking alien. However, the actual process was *extremely* complicated and every department involved in the making of the show was caught up in it, in one way or another. When your 'guest star' for the episode isn't exactly on the set, everyone has to really work to make it look as though he is!

"This character is kind of a Frankenstein creation," Tichenor reveals, further explaining how this very intricate little guy came to

life. "It's actually made up of Teryl Rothery, who did the body performance and the voice (which, naturally, was digitally disguised) augmented by effects from Craig, the lead animator at Image Engine. All of the main body movements — arms and legs, body and torso — was motion capture of Teryl. The finer movements — the fingers, the hands and all the facial expressions — were done by hand by the animators at Image Engine. So while Heimdall doesn't actually look or speak like Teryl, he does move like her. So much so that, for instance, videotapes of Teryl performing the motion capture were used to help animate the Asgard's face.

"It's interesting," Tichenor continues, "because I see so many different people in that character. It's really weird how something that is not alive can look so real, like somebody who is actually standing there. Martin Wood and I were just watching it at lunch time," he grins. "It's marvellous how that character worked; how everybody chipped in to make it turn out so well." With a modest shrug he nods, "So that was the end of season five for us. We made a promise to deliver a creature the like of which hadn't been seen before, and we did it! A lot of times, if the effects don't quite work, you can just edit around them or trim them down a little bit, but in this case we really had to deliver the goods. There was no other way, because Heimdall was the heart and soul of the episode." Laughing about the time and hard work it took to create some seemingly effortless scenes, Tichenor admits, "It felt great being able to do it... but we haven't been able to do it again since! It seems as though Martin Wood would like us to do motion picture-type extravaganzas every episode! It's true though, we just keep getting more and more ambitious. It's always intriguing trying to figure out where we'll go next..." ⅄

Opposite page:
The fully CG Asgard, Heimdall, in 'Revelations'.
Above: *Teryl Rothery, who provided the voice and body movement, wore this Heimdall 'costume' while on set.*

Hair and Make-up

Brad Wright

"Our make-up department produces phenomenal results on a day-to-day basis. They truly deserve every Gemini nomination they've received."

Hair Today...
By Key Hairdresser Patrick O'Brien

Opposite page: The elegantly coiffured Amanda Tapping. Below: Key hairdresser Patrick O'Brien with an extra cast member.

My work day usually starts at approximately 6am, although there are days when I start at the unearthly hour of 4.30am. It all depends on the number of main and extra cast members we have on the day's call sheet, and the time of 'set call', which is when the camera should start rolling for the day's filming. I like to get to the unit at least half an hour before my call time, so I can get my breakfast — a very important start to my day!

The next thing I do is read the parts of the script that are being shot that day, and check with my script breakdown to see if any hair changes are necessary. If some of the day's filming involves a continuation of something we started at an earlier date, I refer to the continuity photos taken at the time we filmed that portion, so I can match the look.

The continuity photos are vital. They're kept in albums, and carefully labelled to indicate which episode they're from. We also use the photos when it comes to getting our recurring characters ready for the camera. There are quite a few characters that return every season, and some will return more than a couple of times within a year. Occasionally a character will return after many years away, for example appearing briefly in the first season, and then coming back in the fifth. In this case I have to go right back to the first season's album, and find the picture of that character. Sometimes the role will be taken by a different person, as in the case of Teal'c's wife, so revising the photos is essential. Taking into account that time has passed (and in the case of Teal'c's wife, her life had been very hard since Teal'c left Abydos), the photos are invaluable to help me get as close as possible to how they would look

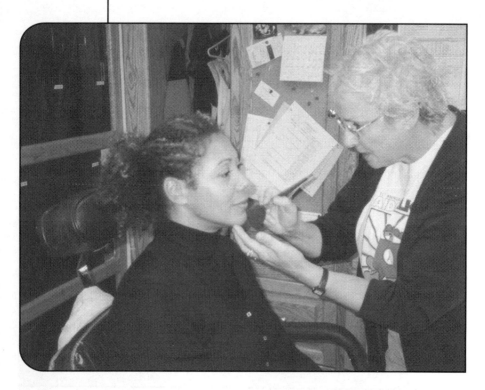

Above: *Make-up supervisor Jan Newman has her work cut out making Thomasina Gibson look glamorous at 5.30am.*

now.

Although we do still use Polaroid cameras in some instances, I take continuity photos with a digital camera these days, and have a lap top computer with a printer, so I can print the previous day's photos in the morning. I find the digital camera gives a more detailed photo than a Polaroid.

Depending on who is in the first scene to be shot that day, we prepare them for camera in priority of appearance. Richard Dean Anderson will occasionally come in and wash his hair at the basin; sometimes he will need a shave, which could be with an electric razor, or a wet shave. Many times he will actually need to look a mess, because the script calls for O'Neill to be in a state of distress, depending on what challenge SG-1 are up against that day. I usually cut his hair at the start of an episode.

Amanda Tapping has her hair cut short of late. She has wonderful bone structure and lovely big eyes, which the shorter hair shows off to a decidedly flattering advantage. Christopher Judge shaves his head for the part, so there's not a lot of styling required there! I clipper cut Don Davis's hair very short, military style, in keeping with his role as General

Hammond.

As well as styling our main actors, my assistant Rose and I also see to it that the additional cast members (as many as twenty to twenty-five at times) are suitably styled for their roles as guest stars and background players. Our job then is to maintain the look throughout the day, and make any changes needed to keep the continuity, also keeping an eye on any script changes (which happen on a daily basis). We often film out of the studio in very heavy rain or sweltering heat, so keeping our actors comfortable and maintaining the look is quite a task! Thankfully, our cast is very easy going and loves to laugh and have fun, so the frequent twelve to fourteen hour days pass with very little stress at all.

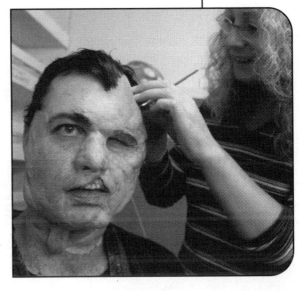

Above: Finishing Nirrti's evil handiwork.

Faking It
By Make-up Supervisor Jan Newman

One of the things I love about working on Stargate is that it's never boring. It seems that each season, each script, each day brings a new challenge for us to undertake, and seasons five and six were no exception. We created so many wonderful make-up effects — some subtle, some rather more prominent — but here are a few of the ones which stick out in my mind as being particularly special.

'Wounding' Teal'c is always a challenge, because black skin generally bruises in quite a different way from white skin. So, when we apply make-up to Christopher Judge to make it look as if Teal'c has been injured, we use darker colours (although we do use quite dark colours on most bruises, depending on how old they are meant to be). When we had to do the bruise Teal'c receives when he's bashed by Apophis at the start of season five, we created the bruise first, then put the cuts over the top. We then highlighted the area so it looked as though he'd just been hit. I think the bruise we see in 'Threshold' is particularly effective.

Midway through season six we got to work with two of my favourite guest stars, Patrick McKenna and John Billingsley, in an episode called

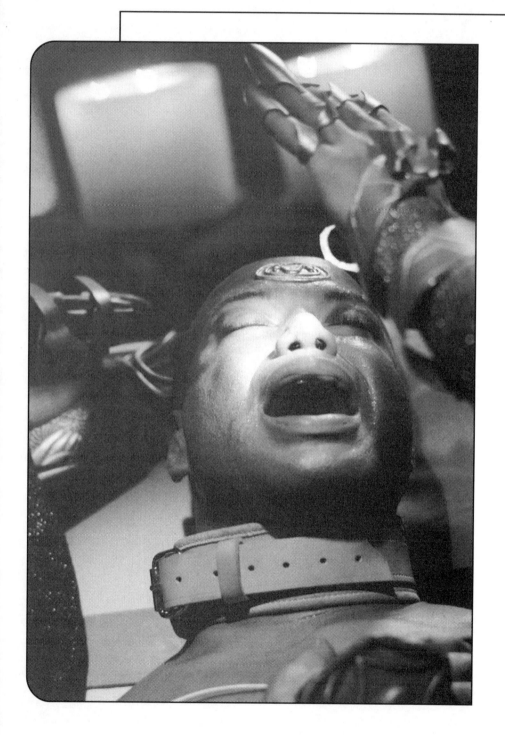

'The Other Guys'. Working with them was a delight, because they'd bounce off one another constantly, and keep us all highly entertained! In the episode, they played two stumblebums trying to save the world. One of the things they had to do was to draw tattoos on themselves in an attempt at disguise. So we had to design tattoos that really looked hand drawn! At one point, John's character had to smudge his. It made me laugh every time I looked at him.

The special effects make-up supremo Todd Masters has created so many wonderful effects for us in the last couple of years. His work on 'Metamorphosis' in particular shows his genius. I can't begin to describe how incredible that was up close. In the episode, Nirrti has altered people's DNA, changing them into horrific creatures. The three main characters were spectacular, but we also had ten background characters, each with their own special touches.

Todd has a very vivid imagination! He designs all his work digitally, on his computer. I remember him printing out the designs for that episode and taking them to the producers, who were naturally blown away. Todd is a truly remarkable man.

On a gentler note, I personally loved 'Ascension', because we got to change Amanda Tapping's look. She was only in uniform for half a day shooting that episode. The rest of the time she was in civvies, so we got to glam her up quite a bit! Instead of having to stick with the regular SG-1 look, we could show how gorgeous she actually is. It was her show, and she did a fantastic job. I loved having the opportunity to show off her natural beauty. It only takes the tiniest bit of powder, and the odd touch of blusher and lip gloss, to make her look even more stunning! ⅄

Opposite page:
A battered and bruised Teal'c.
Above: A smudged John Billingsley.
Pages 148-149:
'Metamorphosis', from production design to finished make-up.

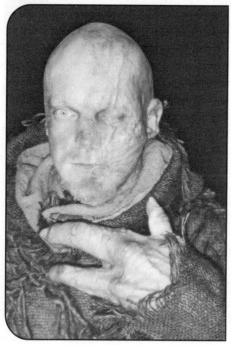

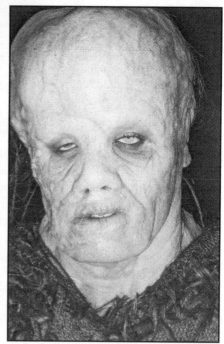

MUSIC

"Joel's music continues to have a huge impact on the quality of *Stargate SG-1*."

E ver wondered why some images on screen can move you to tears, even if there isn't a word being spoken? Or wondered why your heart is speeding up when all you're doing is sitting on the edge of the sofa? Next time, take a moment to listen to the score. If music be the food of love, light-speed and slimy snakeheads, composer and musician Joel Goldsmith is sure to play on. Inspired by some of the symphonic greats of our time, Goldsmith creates his own orchestral masterpieces to further enhance our perception of *Stargate SG-1*, providing the essential finishing touch to episodes of the show.

Goldsmith was no stranger to Brad Wright and Jonathan Glassner, having worked with them on *The Outer Limits* before the call came to provide the all-important musical accompaniment to their latest series. "When Brad and Jonathan started SG-1, they asked me to do the pilot," says Goldsmith. "The score was done orchestrally, based on the original themes from the movie, by David Arnold. But they also let me write my own end title for the show. I was very thrilled and happy to do it."

Since then, Goldsmith has composed many of the stirring pieces that augment the onscreen action, evolving Arnold's themes into the ones we now know and love as exclusively *Stargate SG-1*'s. "For example," explains Goldsmith, "I adapted and expounded on the Jaffa march. David's was very brooding and dramatic, but I specifically wanted something to portray the menace of the soldiers advancing on their prey. I've kept that theme from the beginning of the show right up to the present day." Chuckling, the composer says, "They tell me it's very effective."

Goldsmith's task isn't the easiest in the world, given that he actually lives a thousand miles from where production takes place. But our cunning composer has a tried and tested method for getting each piece of music just right. "First off I get what's called a 'producers cut', which is the first version of an episode that leaves the editing room," he explains. "From that I get a feeling for the show. Then they send me what's called the 'locked print', which is the final version of the episode, although generally it's without the special and visual effects. Robert Cooper, Brad and I then get on the phone, synchronize our video players, watch the show and discuss how we will approach the music. We've been working together this way for so long now that we can practically

read each other's minds, and when I hear their emotion about the show it gets me going too!"

Surprisingly, Goldsmith generally provides most of the practical instrumental skills for each episode he scores. "I play most of the music myself, simulating the orchestra electronically, just bringing in two or three musicians to give that extra sense of authenticity. If I manage to make the audience feel that they are hearing a real, full-size orchestra, then I've done my job."

Having worked on the show from its inception, Goldsmith could be forgiven for feeling a little jaded. Quite the opposite is true, however. "Usually by season four or five of any series, the stories kind of peter out and begin to suck," he grins, "but with this show, things just keep getting better and better!" ʎ

Above: Another dramatic Stargate *moment, accentuated by the score.*

Stargate and the Fans

Amanda Tapping

"Our fans are the most intelligent, loyal, funny and warm-hearted individuals on the planet."

targate fans have proved themselves to be the staunchest and most loyal of groups. They are also some of the warmest, friendliest, most enthusiastic and accommodating people anyone could hope to meet. From Auchermuchter to Zambia, Gaters will congregate in groups, large or small, each meeting typified by masses of laughter and light, and plenty of intelligent conversation — even before the bar has opened. How do I know this? I've been to many of them! But don't just take my word for it. Have a look at this trio of first-hand accounts.

A Report from Gatecon 2002
By Richard Pasco

Gatecon continues to go from strength to strength, attracting attendees from as far afield as the United Kingdom, Canada, the United States, Australia, Germany, Switzerland, Israel, the Netherlands, France, Italy, Spain, Japan, South Africa and New Zealand!

One of the highlights of the last two Gatecon events has been the chance to tour the *Stargate* set, at the Bridge Studios in Vancouver. Having been to the set several times over the last few years, you might think the novelty would wear off, but that's not the case. I never fail to be in awe every time I walk into the Gate Room! Better yet is to watch the expressions of those seeing the Gate up close and personal for the first time. In 2002 we were able to take more than 100 attendees to the studio, where we were given a guided tour that included not only the Gate Room, but also Hammond's office and the Briefing Room, plus the chance to sit in the driving seat of the *Prometheus*. Visitors were also able to take photographs of one another on the ramp in front of a closed Gate, complete with iris and wormhole lighting effect. Accompanied by lighting technician Rick Dean and Noleen Tobin from the art department, attendees were given a unique and in-depth look at what goes on behind the scenes.

Another popular feature of Gatecon is the charity auction, which raises money for the *Make a Wish Foundation*. In 2002, there were dozens of props and costumes from the studio up for grabs, plus many more items donated by individuals. The proceeds from this event were

sufficient to grant an incredible six wishes for children with life-threatening illnesses.

The convention appeared on Canadian television in the form of a series of live broadcasts from the event, linked to an interview with Amanda Tapping back at the TV studio. Gatecon also featured in a behind-the-scenes documentary produced by Star TV.

All in all, Gatecon 2002 was another great success. We look forward to perhaps seeing you in Vancouver for Gatecon 2003!

Teryl Takes Time Out at Cult TV
By Alex J. Geairns

Stargate SG-1 is one of the Top Twenty series of all time, according to a poll carried out amongst attendees of the Cult TV Festival. We were therefore delighted that Teryl Rothery agreed to join us for our mini-vacation in the sleepy seaside town of Southport. It was October 2002, and the traditionally bad English weather couldn't dampen the spirits of any of our twenty celebrity guests, or our enthusiastic holidaymakers.

Page 153: Gatecon 2002 attendees, during their set tour.
Above: *Sam and Martouf, reunited at last! Gatecon guests Amanda Tapping and JR Bourne.*

Guests from *Farscape* to *Captain Scarlet*, from *Monty Python* to *Babylon 5* shared equal billing with the lovely Ms R. Those who work within the television community are always interested in meeting others within that sphere, if only to swap tales and anecdotes. True to her outgoing nature, Teryl loved meeting up with this diverse range of fellow thesps. From my point of view, it was spellbinding to watch her chat not only with her own fans and fans of *Stargate SG-1* but also with those who only had a passing knowledge of the show and her part in it. Friends like Teryl are what make Cult TV special. Those who attend have a genuine interest in all sorts of series, and want to discover what hooks others into appreciating shows they may not have taken to… yet.

Teryl was a gracious ambassador for *Stargate SG-1* throughout the weekend, and apparently just *loves* to shop. Southport's eclectic range of stores was a perfect 'hunting ground'. Like us, the store vendors can't wait for her to come back!

Bottoms up at Blackpool
As described by Brian Cooney

It was raining, freezing and blowing a gale, but the 1,200 attendees who braved the worst of the British weather were warmed to the cockles of their hearts by the shenanigans of the guests who attended the SG5 event in Blackpool last year. Put nine cast members, one executive producer, one locations manager and a roomful of fans together and the key word can only be 'fun'. The highlight of the event for Brian was the "bum squeezing auction" initiated by JR Bourne and

Above: Teryl Rothery takes a break from shopping.

Christopher Judge. This highly amusing and very public display of affection resulted in some lucky soul paying £500 for the privilege of squeezing JR Bourne's pert cheeks! There were lots of other tweaks and shrieks, which combined to result in lots of laughs and, more importantly, literally thousands of pounds being raised for charity.

So there you have it. Just a taste of how much fun these events can be. Next time you see a *Stargate* guest on a convention list, sign up. You'll be in good company, and if you don't have a good time — you must be related to a Goa'uld. **Λ**

Afterword

J ust a few years ago we had only ratings, the occasional review in the press, and the opinions of our families for feedback. Now, it's just a mouse click away. Opinions are posted the moment an episode airs. Some fans will heap praise... others will hate it. Some will really, *really* hate it. (We seem to have a lot of fans who love to hate our show, but as any studio executive will tell you, "It doesn't matter, as long as they watch!") Along with these critiques, there are also recurring questions about why we do things the way we do. Here are the answers to some of them:

Why doesn't the team go off-world every episode? I happen to think some of our best episodes are Earth-based, but even if we wanted to go to a different planet every week, we couldn't do it. Even if we had an unlimited budget to build the sets we'd need to create an alien world for each episode (which we don't!), we have a finite amount of stage space. The art, construction, wardrobe, set decoration and props departments are made up of people who already work twelve to fourteen hour days. For every 'Full Circle' we make, we need to shoot a couple of

Earth-based episodes to offset the financial and personal toll of creating alien planets on a television budget.

Why are there so many trees on other planets? For practical reasons, we are forced to shoot on Earth, more specifically, in the vicinity of Vancouver, British Columbia. We've pulled off a handful of minor miracles over the years to create the exteriors of worlds without trees — the desert of Abydos for example is an ever-shrinking postage stamp of land just south of the city — but most of the rest of the province is forest. It's one of my pet peeves too.

Why do some episodes stand alone, without contributing to the arc of the series? The more serialised a television show becomes, the more difficult it is for new or occasional viewers to appreciate that show. On the other hand, a series that resets to zero at the end of every episode doesn't reward its viewers. I like a balance between the two, and that's what I've tried to maintain.

How could you just end it like that...? Occasionally, certain events are left to take place in the imagination of the viewer. The endings of 'Last Stand' or 'Abyss' for example, leave the viewer with the knowledge of what will happen, without actually showing it. Many fans complained that they'd been cheated, as though we had somehow failed to record events that had actually taken place, or worse, ran short of time, leaving these scenes on the cutting room floor. Rest assured, if we ever commit the impossibly large resources required to shoot scenes like these, they'll make the final cut.

Why did you kill off my favourite character? There are different reasons for each case, but most often, it's to serve the story. It also serves to increase suspense in the subsequent episodes... in a dangerous situation, anything can happen. After all, it's our job to entertain. Sometimes that means moving an audience to laughter, and sometimes it means moving an audience to tears.

Previous page:
Richard Dean Anderson ponders the second question.
Above: *Brad Wright.*

Why don't you bring back all those great writers from the early seasons? Every writer that is not currently on staff has been re-written — often completely — by either myself, or Rob Cooper (since Jonathan left). Occasionally it's just a polish, but often we have to start again at page one. That's the way it works. Some of my best work on *Stargate* has somebody else's name on it. On many shows, the showrunner types put their own names on the script as well. I don't believe in doing that.

Why don't you listen to the fans more? We *do* listen. Then we make the show the way we think it should be made. There's just no other way to make television.

Who is your favourite writer? Thomasina Gibson, of course!

Brad Wright
Executive Producer *Stargate SG-1*

About the author

Thomasina Gibson trained as a schoolteacher, but decided to develop her love of theatre by moving to Stratford Upon Avon, working at the Royal Shakespeare Theatre for several seasons. She then joined British Airways as a cabin crew member, and later spent three years at the BBC. Having taken a long break to raise two children, she returned to writing, initially as a hobby, and now writes for a number of film and television magazines in the UK and US. She also contributes to SCI.FI.com, the official website for the SCI FI Channel. Away from the genre, she has contributed news and sports features to the *Daily Telegraph* and lifestyle and television features to the *Daily Express*. A huge fan of cult television and film, Gibson has worked as consultant on several sci-fi/cult-related shows, including the BBC's *Lost in Space* and Channel 4's factual documentary *Riddle of the Skies*. She is also proud to have worked as an associate producer on several "added value" reports for MGM's *Stargate SG-1* DVDs. Gibson is currently working with HTV Young Person's Workshops, co-producing a documentary highlighting teenage film-makers travelling abroad. ⋏

Below: Stuart Gibson (front),with (left to right) Thomasina Gibson, Amanda Tapping, Michael Shanks and Alexis Cruz, on the set of 'Full Circle'.

PEOPLE OF THE TAU'RI ...

... join us at the largest gathering on Earth of cast, crew & fans
in celebration of the hit TV show STARGATE SG-1

11 - 14 September 2003

Best Western Richmond Inn Vancouver – Canada

Teryl Rothery ~ Don S Davis
JR Bourne ~ Jay Acovone ~ Douglas Arthurs
Colin Cunningham
plus more guests to be announced

convention highlights include:

City Tour to Filming Locations

Charity Auction   Autograph Sessions

Photograph Sessions   Stargate Merchandise

Cocktail Party   Costume Contest

plus lots more

We can also handle your reservation for a room at the convention hotel
Car Rental discounts for convention attendees

Gatecon supports the Make a Wish Foundation

GATECON 2003

WWW.GATECON.COM